A Manager's Guide to **Staff Incentives** *and Performance Improvement Techniques*

John G. Fisher

YOURS TO HAVE AND TO HOLD
BUT NOT TO COPY

The publication you are reading is protected by copyright law. This means that the publisher could take you and your employer to court and claim heavy legal damages if you make unauthorised photocopies from these pages. Photocopying copyright material without permission is no different from stealing a magazine from a newsagent, only it doesn't seem like theft.

The Copyright Licensing Agency (CLA) is an organisation which issues licences to bring photocopying within the law. It has designed licensing services to cover all kinds of special needs in business, education and government.

If you take photocopies from books, magazines and periodicals at work your employer should be licensed with CLA. Make sure you are protected by a photocopying licence.

The Copyright Licensing Agency Limited, 90 Tottenham Court Road, London, W1P 0LP. Tel: 0171 436 5931. Fax: 0171 436 3986.

First published in 1996

Apart from any fair dealing for the purposes of research or private study, or criticism or review, as permitted under the Copyright, Designs and Patents Act, 1988, this publication may only be reproduced, stored or transmitted, in any form or by any means, with the prior permission in writing of the publishers, or in the case of reprographic reproduction in accordance with the terms and licences issued by the CLA. Enquiries concerning reproduction outside those terms should be sent to the publishers at the undermentioned address:

Kogan Page Limited
120 Pentonville Road
London N1 9JN

© John G Fisher, 1996

British Library Cataloguing in Publication Data

A CIP record for this book is available from the British Library.

ISBN 0 7494 1600 9

Typeset by BookEns Ltd, Royston, Herts.
Printed in England by Clays Ltd, St Ives plc

CONTENTS

Acknowledgements   6

1. The Profit Potential   7
Improving performance   7
Where should you begin?   9
Specific incremental profit   11

2. The Human Audit   15
Human audit guidelines   16
Company performance   17
Personnel inventory   19
Digging deeper   25
Understanding job roles in detail   27
Recruiting the decision-makers   28
Taking an overall view   29
Testing your presentation   30

3. Constructing the programme   33
Motivation theory   34
Isolating the objectives   38
Quantitative objectives   40
Incentive techniques for individual participants   42
Variations for team participants   49
How long should the incentive programme last?   50
Rules and regulations   53

4. Building the Budget — 55
The concept of incremental profit 56
Cost headings 58

5. Cash or Non-Cash, That is the Question — 63
Basic salary 64
Salary plus commission 65
Performance related pay (PRP) 69
Money – the worst motivator 70

6. Flexible Benefits — 77
Benefits as security 78
Benefits as loyalty incentives 79
The consultation process 85
The stages of effective communication 92
Tax, insurance and financial planning issues 93
Administration 96
Is choice of benefits motivational? 99

7. Incentive Travel: Everyone's Top Reward — 101
Extraordinary rewards 101
Promising the earth 103
Making incentive travel different 109
Trends in incentive travel 120
Individual incentive travel 121
Significant product factors 122
Other means of transport 123
Forward planning of destinations 126
A final word about purchasing 127

8. Merchandise — 129
Merchandise catalogues 129
Invent your own catalogue! 135

9. Vouchers — 139
Vouchers *v* merchandise 139
Advantages of vouchers 140
Redeeming features 142
Disadvantages of vouchers 143
Administration 144
Voucher promotion 145

'Designer awards' 145
Developing technology 146

10. Events **149**
Conferences 150
Weekend incentives 156
Group activities 157
Staff parties 159

11. Measure, Monitor, Mirror **161**
How to measure performance 161
Measure 163
Monitor 169
Mirror 172

12. Recognition Systems **175**
Why recognition works 175
Types of corporate recognition 176
Club concepts 177
Distributor clubs 178
Frequent buyer/loyalty programmes 179
Informal recognition 179

13. Performance Improvement: The Future **183**

Index **185**

ACKNOWLEDGEMENTS

I am grateful to the many business colleagues who have helped me formulate 'best practice' over the last 15 years. Among them are some specific people and companies I would like to thank for their invaluable contribution to this book.

To Ron MacDonald, Roger Dolphin and Nick Throp at Sedgwick Noble Lowndes and Russ Watling at Mercury Communications for their help with the chapter on Flexible Benefits.

In addition, to the following people who provided case history material: Gary Lubner, Autoglass; Charles Hunter-Pease, Volvo; Eric Mesnil, Everest (Paris); Mario Sciacca, Promoplan (Milan); Business Incentives Inc. (USA); Tony Patience, formerly at AEG; Bruce Bolger, independent consultant and everyone at Page & Moy Marketing.

Finally, I am grateful to Touche Ross for their permission to reproduce statistics from their European Incentive and Business Travel Meeting Survey, augmenting the chapter on Incentive Travel.

1

THE PROFIT POTENTIAL

Most people exert only 15 per cent of their combined intelligence, skills and aptitudes in their employment.
William James

IMPROVING PERFORMANCE

The corporate goal of every business is to survive. If it can make a profit at the same time, even better.

But a company by itself does not make profits. People do. The sum total of all the employees' efforts creates the wealth which allows the company to invest in new systems, products and services for its future survival. So, doing business in the long term is the process of people improving their performance at work.

But how many employees ever reach their potential at their place of work? Almost everyone has the capacity to perform better, whether they do the wordprocessing or create company policy. Individual one-to-one coaching can help but the most cost-effective solution is a group programme, whether for 50 or 5000 participants.

The regular use of team or group performance improvement programmes and incentives can help you identify what your current operating standards are, and what capacity for improvement there may be. You can then improve those standards through specific training, better internal communication and appropriate rewards to create incremental profit at every level in the business.

But does it work?

Staff Incentives and Performance Management Techniques

Volvo

Early in 1986 Volvo UK were concerned about the diminishing returns they were achieving using cash sums for dealers as an incentive to sell cars. They were two years away from being able to introduce a replacement model for the then mature 300 series small car, but they still needed sales now.

It was decided that a mixture of cash and non-cash incentives should be used for the first time to stimulate sales. Dealers were given a specific target with mid-campaign awards of luxury Orient Express baggage. Fifty top dealers were to be rewarded with a lavish incentive trip on the Venice–Simplon Orient Express with two further nights in Venice, staying at the Danieli Hotel. Salespeople received a selection of retail vouchers for each car sold.

The results were astounding. Car sales market share for the second quarter leapt from 2.66 per cent the previous year to 4.75 per cent, giving the importers, Lex Service PLC, a 23 per cent increase in imported cars over the previous year.

The performance improvement was reported prominently in the *Financial Times* on 6 June 1986.

Autoglass

Autoglass are Europe's leading car window replacement company. In 1992, Autoglass UK embarked on a performance improvement programme for all 2000 UK staff. After considerable analysis of job types and historical performance patterns, staff were categorised into four key areas: distribution, central control (telesales), head office and branches.

Each job task was analysed to identify specific areas of performance improvement: customer perception of service; distribution errors; clerical errors; repairs achieved. An historical standard was set for each task and improvements were measured. Rewards in the form of retail vouchers were offered for individual performance against these criteria.

Performance improved significantly in many areas:

1. The number of 'abandoned calls' (customers who hang up because they were kept waiting too long by the telephonist) fell from 3.5 to 1 per cent.

2. The average number of clerical errors in customer documentation fell from 20 to 5 per cent.
3. Customer complaints fell from 12 to 7.5 per cent.
4. The Customer Opinion Index rose significantly.

The programme enabled Autoglass to move from a customer-reactive organisation to a customer-service organisation with a significant positive increase in the perception of Autoglass by consumers.

SNCF (French Railways)

SNCF – the national French rail system – needed to introduce confident usage of a new ticketing system (SOCRATES) for customers, and at the same time to instil the idea in over 7000 employees that making sales and keeping customers was important.

It was decided after extensive analysis that 30 per cent of performance should be knowledge based, with the remaining 70 per cent based on sales. Nine key objectives were distinguished on which comic strip training modules were based (starting a conversation, talking to clients while using the system, deciding the best ticket option, offering discounts where appropriate). The awards were based on merchandise by mail order or a choice of retail vouchers for successful attainment of leagued thresholds across 23 separate rail regions. There were three levels of reward in each of the three categories of home, leisure and hi-fi/video, totalling 93 specific items presented in a loose-leaf catalogue format.

Sales volume increased significantly in all regions but of more importance with such a long-term investment was the considerable and identifiable improvement in technical fluency with the new ticketing system.

WHERE SHOULD YOU BEGIN?

- **Offer more money**   You could take this option but as you will see later, money is an expensive way to incentivise or reward behavioural change. Offering more money may change the speed at which people work but it does not, in isolation, solve the problem of lack of focus or inefficient working practices. Nor does it instil sincere loyalty.

Staff Incentives and Performance Management Techniques

- **Change employee benefits** You could change the way you pay employee benefits. With costs of 30 per cent or more going largely unnoticed for each employee, you may decide that many of the traditional benefits which are offered, such as life assurance, pensions or private health care no longer represent good value for money.
- **Provide non-cash rewards** You could decide to offer one-off awards for specific performance improvement. But what should the awards be? A trophy? A certificate? More luncheon vouchers? A meal for two? Or even a weekend in Paris? If you decide to reward one department or one grade of employee, what about all the others?
- **Provide incentive travel** Incentive travel is by far the most popular non-cash incentive. Companies who earmark a budget for incentives regularly spend considerable sums on overseas incentive travel. The UK estimate for 1994 was £500 million. In the US industry estimates are as high as £4000 million. Is this the most effective use of any given budget? Do participants actually work harder or are you simply rewarding the predictable top echelon? Even if you are convinced it works, how should you decide which venue to choose, what kind of programme to run once you get there, and how do you make the most efficient use of hotels, airlines and all the other supplier services, who are part of the incentive travel product?
- **A merchandise catalogue** Perhaps a range of merchandise would be more suitable or better still store vouchers so that winners can choose what they want. With the move towards more personal freedom in all walks of life, perhaps some system of electronic credit might be more appropriate.
- **Recognition systems** Then there is always the question of recognition, not only for specific achievements during the year, but for consistently high performance over the full year or even over the length of a career in the form of long service awards. Are such items effective? What is the best way to use them in a complex company where people perform a wide range of different functions?

Measuring performance standards

Most important of all is the question of setting standards and monitoring individual performance. Within a sales environment it is relatively easy to track sales performance, but with the increasing emphasis on quality and consumer accountability, what quality measures could you introduce to provide the correct cocktail of checks and balances? What about staff who apparently have no output? Once defined, you need to set up systems to monitor progress. Sometimes the cost of monitoring may outweigh the financial benefits of higher performance, so how can you refine the scheme to deliver a balanced result and a bottom-line, incremental profit? Then you need to decide how to communicate performance to participants.

Deciding what to invest

Deciding what represents an appropriate budget to promote performance improvement is a discipline in itself. Many industries set themselves a percentage of turnover. Others set a fixed budget. However, the most efficient way to set a budget is based on the incremental profit the additional activity will generate. The assumptions and estimates will be different for each situation, even within the same company. To start the whole process off, you need to identify an overall financial aim, so that the fixed costs of promotion are appropriate to the variable cost of achieving the improvement. In some situations you may decide no amount of money will ever change the outcome significantly.

Bearing in mind all these problems and the variable nature of the choices that can be made, is it all worth it?

SPECIFIC INCREMENTAL PROFIT

Experience with clients new to performance improvement and those who have been using motivation programmes for many years shows that identifiable additional profits are generated. But no single technique works in isolation. Often, the true benefits come from synergy: sales working with support staff; separate subsidiaries sharing a common database; tailored schemes for junior and senior staff; layered incentives for different levels; the development of new communication channels. Companies that use many or all the techniques in this book have done so for some time and will continue in the future for as long as they can show an additional benefit to the shareholders and employees alike.

Staff Incentives and Performance Management Techniques

Within the performance improvement area one thing is certain. A business will not improve until the performance of the people it employs improves. The challenge is to unlock that potential for the company's benefit and create job roles which are more fulfilling.

The additional profit potential is enormous. Almost all companies claim they undertake some type of performance improvement activity and from the small collection of published case histories and anecdotal evidence, improvements can represent additional turnover anywhere between 5 and 50 per cent, sometimes even more, for a minimal outlay.

But these techniques should not only be applied to the business world. In August 1994 Professor Michael Barber of Keele University released the results of a survey of attitudes among 10,000 young people at school. It revealed a general lack of motivation among 40 per cent of pupils with up to 20 per cent of 16 year olds truanting regularly. Between 30 and 40 per cent claimed they would rather not go to school. Seventy per cent said they counted the minutes to the end of most lessons. This waste of young human potential to improve is enormous.

This guide is intended to help managers tap into the vast human resource within their company and exploit the natural desire for improvement. Few people deliberately set out to perform poorly. With the right environment, developing a 'performance improvement' culture can make a significant contribution to better bottom-line profits, and a more empowered and enthusiastic workforce.

SUMMARY

- Most employees have the capacity to improve their performance.
- There are many examples of incremental profit using performance improvement techniques.
- Incentives range from cash, benefits and vouchers to merchandise, travel and even recognition for a job well done.
- The true benefits come from synergy between participating groups or departments.
- Developing a performance improvement culture is the key to a more productive workforce.

2

THE HUMAN AUDIT

The answer is not separate from the problem
Krishnamurti

A performance improvement programme cannot be built on the basis of a few chance conversations and a hundred sets of luggage. If it could, improving performance would be much easier and much more common. You need to consider in great detail whom you are trying to motivate, how they operate within the wider context of the company and what practical measures can be put in place to monitor performance.

But research, in motivation terms, is not about anonymous consumers. You start with what you know, namely your own industry, your own company history, your own people, your own objectives.

It is going to mean a considerable commitment of time spent at head office and around the branches or local offices rummaging through personnel files, sales records, commission statements, historical company performance and asking specific people a few important questions. Inevitably you will find that the vital pieces of information are missing or have never been collected in the way you want them. You will get considerable resistance from every department who will at first be suspicious of your intentions. After all, why bother to investigate motivation when everyone knows that money is the only thing that motivates people to work harder? (See Chapter 5 to find out if it does.)

But before you start collecting data, consider carefully whether

Staff Incentives and Performance Management Techniques

what you are collecting will be relevant when you come to assess opportunities for performance improvement.

Here are some research guidelines which will be useful, but there may be other records relevant to your company situation. Leave no stone unturned.

HUMAN AUDIT GUIDELINES

1. Analyse company performance over the previous five years in terms of sales, profits and return on investment. Pay particular attention to any mergers, acquisitions, legislation or economic factors which could have seriously affected the overall bottom-line position. It does not need to be an exhaustive financial assessment or 100 per cent accurate. You're trying to get a broad snapshot of growth, stasis or decline, both in isolation and against the background of your industry. You may need to do this by division or by product group.
2. Classify and quantify what personnel you have, and summarise their impact on company growth. It is important to clarify, perhaps for the first time, each group's strategic task and value to the company, and describe those tasks in simple language.
3. Within the sales function identify the distribution of sales per salesperson, month by month – to get the cyclical pattern – and the overall distribution of individual performance (10 per cent above £50K, 25 per cent below £20K etc). Drawing a distribution graph helps.
4. Within the administrative function, clarify any objective measures of performance, such as retention rates, absenteeism and skill requirements you think could be improved on, given the current recruitment policy or local job market. You may also wish to consider overhead costs as a percentage of revenue to see which way the trend is leading.
5. Catalogue all previous attempts at 'motivating' any teams, groups or divisions of the company, together with any data on improved performance, accurate or spurious.
6. Talk to all department heads in general terms about morale, motivation, performance standards and incentives, with the aim of agreeing a broad statement of the prevailing views. What they perceive to be the current state of play is more useful than what they feel ought to be the case.

When this is done, you will be in a position to do some reliable, objective research. Then and only then can you start planning the programme.

COMPANY PERFORMANCE

But let's go back a few steps. It is not your job to make a full marketing analysis of the industry or your own performance in it. If you are an established company, such a report probably exists already. The watchword is simplicity.

The sort of measures you should be looking for are:

1. turnover (sales);
2. net profit (before tax);
3. return on investment;
4. inflation/interest rates in the economy;
5. industry growth/decline rates;
6. product trends/market take-up of new products.

The result will be a general statement of the health of the industry and your company's performance within that industry. This will be the background to the need for better motivation or, at the very least, the cultural acceptability that higher performance could make a difference. You need to be honest about the current culture before taking the project even to the stage of initial field research. Big companies are full of project teams designing apples when what the directors want is oranges or pears – or to get out of market gardening altogether. Your research will help to isolate the main barriers to higher individual and team performance.

Senior management attitudes

The attitude of the key directors in the company cannot be overstated. If your company has never been involved in a centralised motivation programme the idea of starting one may be perceived as a significant financial risk, which means you will need the enthusiastic support of the company 'power brokers', particularly the financial director who, if the budgets are significant, should buy into the incremental benefit argument to defend any scaling down of the initial investment.

Staff Incentives and Performance Management Techniques

In a CBI (Confederation of British Industry) survey 70 chief executives identified staff morale and motivation to be one of four significant factors in the success of their business. So, you need a statement from the head of the business, one from the head of sales, one from human resources and one from the financial function to support the initiative. It is likely that you will be asking for up to 10 per cent of the post-tax remuneration budget to create the programme, so you need friends in high places to agree those kinds of resources.

But you also need to be honest about whether introducing fully measured performance improvement systems will reap the rewards you expect. Traditionally, in the UK and Europe, motivation schemes have been used on a consistent basis by relatively few predictable industry sectors. Touche Ross, a leading British firm of accountants, conducted a research exercise for EIBTM (European Incentive and Business Travel Meeting) in 1990, covering global trends in the use of incentive travel. One section dealt with which industry is most likely to buy incentive schemes or motivation programmes, on a consistent and regular basis. The answer was as follows.

Table 2.1 Who Uses Incentives?

Type	% of Respondents
Pharmaceuticals	10
Financial services (including insurance companies)	10
Cars	10
Automotive parts	9
Computing	9
Toiletries/cosmetics	9
Electronics	8
Electrical appliances	7
Office equipment	6
Farm equipment	5
Retail	5
Building materials	5
Heating/air conditioning	4
Leisure/catering	1
Other	2
	100%

Source: EITS 1990 Touche Ross

I quote this not to suggest that no other sector considers performance improvement as a means to increased efficiency. They do. But from my own experience, very few companies who are not in the above sectors do so on a regular, planned basis. The relatively low use by retail outlets of staff motivation schemes is perhaps one reason why the customer service reputation of many UK retail personnel is so poor. One element is clearly the margin in the product. Cars, pharmaceuticals, computers and life insurance all benefit from a high margin, thereby making it possible to invest more of the accrued profit for long-term investment in staff who can create repeat purchase and word-of-mouth recommendations.

Things do change over the years. For years banks have had a fearsome reputation for adopting a master–servant approach to customer service. But in recent times enormous resources have been ploughed back into the customer relationship as the banks began to realise that no one stays with one bank for life any more. As in most industries the response has been forced upon them by fierce competition, the general growth in consumer awareness and freedom of choice. By voting with their feet, consumers have forced the banks into a radical rethink of their customer relationships. That means looking carefully at staff performance when they come into contact with customers.

If you are in an industry that does not currently use performance improvement techniques on a regular basis, you may have to work a little harder than your counterpart in the automotive industry or the financial services sector to establish a sound cost/benefit analysis which is one reason why a thorough appraisal of current top level attitudes within the company is so necessary.

PERSONNEL INVENTORY

The next task is a detailed analysis of the personnel you intend to motivate.

How many are there? Are they employed, self-employed, franchisees, part-time? What profile is each group or sub group? Do you consider the profile differences to be significant in terms of motivation? Age? Sex? Length of service? Grade or status within their group? Current earnings?

Questions to ask about sales networks

Here is an example of a personnel survey for an automotive company and a pharmaceutical company. They are both involved in sales to a lesser or greater degree.

Table 2.2 Two Salesforce Profiles

	Automotive dealer principals	Pharmaceutical representatives
Number	300	45
Age range	average 49	average 31
Sex	95% male	55% female
Education	Secondary	Degree, PhD
Location	National (not Rep of Ireland)	Midlands, South
Status	Franchisee principals	Employed consultants
Service	20 years, average	4 years, average
Earnings	£35K, to £110K, average £48K	£25K–£45K

You will see from the comparison that a scheme to motivate one group may not be appropriate for the other group. But avoid thinking of solutions at this stage. You need to concentrate on the analysis so that their primary job functions come into sharp focus.

Strategic role

You should then state the strategic role of each group within the business. We can all agree that new business has an important part to play in the ongoing viability of a company, but what proportion should it represent? For example in some industries repeat business can be as high as 90 per cent, so the role of the salesforce may be largely representation to existing clients. In other industries, new business can be as high as 40 or 50 per cent of total sales turnover. In this case the performance improvement plan needs to reflect this requirement to generate new sales each year from new or existing customers.

Retention

You may need to look at projected retention rates for specific work groups, especially if the industry has in the past operated on relatively high recruitment/low retention ratios. Whatever scheme you eventually devise could be very different if you discover that in any 12-month period 50 per cent of those who start the period do not make it to the end of your performance cycle. More importantly, what about all the new people who have joined since the programme started? How will they be incorporated and at what level of reward or measurement? Should they even be included? If not, how will their job performance be affected if they are excluded indefinitely from an incentive or reward programme?

Distribution

You may have several categories of sales distribution working in a complementary manner. Financial services is a good example of this. A bank, for example, may have its own direct salesforce selling cold to new prospects or warm to introduced leads from its branch network. They may also have an advisory arm which sells products to independent intermediaries (brokers). Or they may have staff within branches who take the initial enquiry and qualify it for other salespeople to follow up and convert, depending on the products being offered or the current legislation of financial services. Each distribution arm needs a specific approach when it comes to performance improvement.

Representatives

Within the automotive industry, there will be salespeople with franchised dealerships but also an employed field or zone salesforce who market the manufacturer's package of products and services to the franchisees. They can be a vital part of the motivational mix as they are often the front-line for the manufacturer when it comes to promotion and acceptability of the programme. (They are also invaluable in providing relevant street-wise feedback on whether the scheme is working the way you wanted it to work.)

Tracking sales

Most businesses have some cyclical trend. Twenty-five per cent of all new car sales fall in August. Peak month for pension sales is March. Toy sales peak in December. Knowledge of the peaks as well as the troughs can determine not only when to launch the programme but when to boost any reward credits in the scheme and when to cut back. In complex business-to-business situations, such as the completion of a large IT (information technology) system sale to a multinational, you need to decide at what moment you perceive the sale to have been made so you can confirm a fair allocation of the credit due. You may even decide with some types of contract sales that credit is minimal, because the sale is often a company team effort led from the very top. So credit is given for opening the door or the quality of the process which resulted in the contract rather than the eventual income generated from the sale itself.

Profile and geographic distribution

You need to analyse what proportion of the salesforce brings in the bulk of the sales, split between existing and new if relevant. In other words, does the 80/20 rule (where 80 per cent of sales are produced by 20 per cent of the people) work for you? A further sophistication could be an analysis of geographic distribution. This may reveal nothing other than a match with the general population distribution. But you may surprise yourself. One London-based life insurance company I worked with had a tremendously successful Scottish operation. To a casual observer, this could be put down to a forceful, enthusiastic regional manager. After a bit of digging, I discovered it was more due to the fact that the company was originally based in Scotland when it was founded some 50 years before, and the relatives and descendants of those early policyholders were still very much alive, kicking and paying their premiums on the dot each month.

Questions to ask about those who do not sell

People who don't sell generally tend to be more difficult to classify and analyse. With salespeople you can always look at their figures. With administrative and management groups judgement can be much more subjective about their performance or attitudes to motivation techniques. Why do you need to know anyway? Surely administrative staff are simply there to do their job? If they do, they stay, if they don't, they get fired. The problem in many companies is that they may not be performing, but still don't get fired. The waste can be calculated and is enormous, even with the most rudimentary accounting system. In practice support staff are usually the group that make the biggest performance improvement of all,

The Human Audit

supporting the received wisdom (and the clinically researched truth) that given the right cultural environment, most people will strive to do better.

What types of non-sales staff are there?

1. The factory or processing unit.
2. Clerical.
3. Junior executives.
4. Managers.
5. Departmental heads.
6. Directors.

Depending on your type of business you may even use a number of consultants who will not be employees, but will still have a strong influence on operational morale and task performance.

Analysing the profile of people in the factory or processing unit could be an eternal task. The numbers, types of worker and the complexity of many large companies can make this job very daunting. (This is one reason why few large companies even attempt it.) But do not forget what we're looking for – a general feel for the status quo with some clues as to how to improve job performance in the future. Understanding what part they play in the creation of the product, including the main procedures they follow, is what you need to concentrate on.

The Tennessee Valley Authority (TVA)

The Tennessee Valley Authority (TVA) is a US government-owned electric utility. With increasing competition and the need to keep existing customers satisfied the TVA developed 'The Quality Alliance' with its key distributors, internal managers and customer service centres. In essence, the company went through a Total Quality Management programme which helped work groups to analyse their work processes and define what quality should be in their particular department. Part of the process was the development of a Customer Satisfaction Index to indicate areas for improvement in the future. In the words of the director of member and employee services, Frank Jennings, 'The Quality Alliance offers a fresh new approach to customer satisfaction as well as bringing pride and excitement back to the power distributor and its employees'.

But without a thorough understanding of what each work group does, such levers for performance improvement can never be developed.

Absenteeism

Looking at processing teams brings its own basket of typical problems which needs measuring in order to decide, eventually, which ones to tackle first. Absenteeism is the most obvious symptom of poor performance, and managers in human resources will be fully aware of techniques to improve the ratio. However, although absenteeism rates overall in the UK have remained static at around 5 per cent over the past ten years, less than half of UK employers bother to question absentees when they return to work. Only 12 per cent reward 100 per cent attendance in the workplace. It is often a social problem in addition to a company problem. When you analyse job functions, whether the operatives are building a car or processing credit card transactions, it is clear that job enrichment has not been thought through. One reason why so many bank processing staff are part-time could be the tedious nature of the processing tasks they are asked to perform. No one could stand to do it on a full-time basis. The late 20th-century world of work is a strange mixture of Victorian monotony and futuristic data manipulation. So much is accomplished, but at what price to the minds of modern day 'mill-workers'? There is much that could be organised for higher job enrichment. But until we have analysed what procedures constitute acceptable job performance, we cannot begin to change it for the better.

After absenteeism, you may look at the exit interviews. But take care not to assume everyone leaves for more money in the next town. Retention factors reveal more about the way staff are managed than the staff themselves. They are the equivalent of the supermarket checkout. Employees often take their basket of complaints about poor management with them when they leave. The remaining managers count the cost in terms of replacement and retraining.

Grievances

Another area to consider is the number of grievances brought to the supervisors or managers as a general measure of satisfaction.

You have to take a view whether the levels are affected in any way by economic factors such as recession. People tend to complain less if they are busy and business is expanding. At this initial stage talk to the supervisors and managers on a one-to-one basis, but listen carefully. They may not be used to talking so frankly about how they feel about job performance, especially if there is any perception that you are 'spying' on their activity levels. They will be used to work study programmes and may expect you to simply set them higher productivity targets. What they will not readily recognise is any probing about motivation or ways to increase job satisfaction. You may find a fair degree of complacency, self-satisfaction, and an unwillingness to admit that the current way of organising and rewarding work is anything other than inevitable. Collect any examples you can of procedures being done that on the face of it seem wasteful of resources or create unnecessary paperwork. Such legacies can be swept away if the analysis of the job roles is carried out correctly.

Morale check

Some companies operate a regular internal morale audit to ensure that company issues such as structural changes, procedures or new products are being handled correctly by managers. This information will be useful to the performance improvement/incentives manager in highlighting specific problems.

DIGGING DEEPER

Your next task may require more devious tactics. In the mid 1970s I used to deal with a direct marketing printing company which specialised in personalised home stationery such as letterheads, labels, envelopes. The research task was to discover what made consumers order certain formats. It was a straightforward job. However, the answers coming out of the advertising agency were based on consumer response and perceived preferences for certain products. In other words, the analysis was based on what sold best. A sound way to progress, in theory.

I decided to spend a day wandering around the client's factory. In particular I was interested to talk to the team that actually fulfilled the orders and reported the figures through to the board. Holding sway was a real swashbuckling 69-year-old chum of the chairman who spent overlong on lunches with his paper merchants and was looking forward to retreating to the golf course full time once his contract was over. It did not take long to discover that he had been briefing his 'girls' to switch consumers to processes which required easier production as he was finding the new techniques a bit of a mystery to buy in. He would get consumers to agree to an alternative paper colour on the basis of a 5 per cent reduction. In fact, he only ever carried two of the six colours advertised because he felt it was all too confusing and expensive to stock so much paper on the basis of potential future orders.

After an hour's discussion with the women who administered the orders it transpired that whatever the advertising agency put in the ads (and they tested them mercilessly), they just fulfilled the orders in the same old way and had done for years.

So, investigating what the actual workers said and did proved more revealing than analysing any number of sales reports and customer coupons. Within a month, the personalised stationery product was revamped, the manager put out to grass and more clerks were taken on to respond to the demand from eager consumers wanting to use their lilac paper (with matching envelopes).

The same technique should apply when it comes to investigating previous motivation schemes. You should start with those who formulated the schemes and implemented them. They will undoubtedly have records of when they were, what awards were made and what effect they had on job performance or general morale. But you need to go beyond this. You need to talk to some long-in-the-tooth participants who will have absolute recall of any oddities or absurdities in the presentation, the rules or the reward fulfilment.

During one such investigation for a client, I discovered that one year the sales director had completely forgotten to organise the regional lunches which were meant to be low level rewards to the locally based administration staff for their part in a sales drive. What made it worse was the fact that he was actually in La Manga with the top sales qualifiers on the same day the clerical winners were expecting to sit down for a well-deserved lunch.

Even good sales figures can be misleading without talking to the actual participants. Many motivation programmes suffer from an excellent launch followed by minimal follow through. This means that invariably the programme fails to get general acceptance. More and more money is arbitrarily thrown at the campaign in the form of additional awards, to the extent that in the last month of the scheme, merely being in employment brought you some kind of credit. So the increase in performance was bought at a heavy price which is not necessarily included in the official campaign records, thereby skewing any objective assessment as to its effectiveness.

UNDERSTANDING JOB ROLES IN DETAIL

A common failing with staff schemes (as opposed to sales incentives) is a lack of research into what people's jobs are and hence what they should be measured on.

We undertook an assignment for a national road and rail distribution company. They had all the latest communication technology, an enviable fleet of cars, lorries and motorbikes, and an excellent relationship with the national rail network. What they did not have was any detailed description of what their people actually did. It was true that every job holder had a job description which spelled out clearly what they were supposed to be doing. The reality was somewhat different.

Our task was to explain to the staff the basis of their monthly cash bonuses. An amount was added to pay cheques based on a complicated financial formula known only to the personnel department. We recommended that, rather than try to explain the formula, we should look at the process. The result was a hands-on analysis of each job holder's key tasks and an agreement to reward each aspect with specific credits. Those credits were translated into cash with a statement showing performance achievement against the agreed minimum standards. Now that the recipients understood what they were being measured on, they could take practical steps to improve their performance and improve their cash bonus in future.

Post-programme research is unlikely to exist in most non-sales schemes. It is often the case that if no one complained the programme was deemed to be a success. Any scheme worth doing in the first place is worth researching when it is all over. To find objective judgements on whether it worked is well-nigh impossible in the absence of any post-programme report so you may have to take an educated guess on its impact, which is not helpful when planning future initiatives.

One illuminating truism which will undoubtedly crop up will be that the lowest paid section of staff are rarely incentivised with anything other than money, middle management are offered share options and the top salespeople go to Rio. Do not despair. By building a description of what each peer group contributes to the process you will be able to identify what element of performance to highlight and provide the most appropriate reward.

RECRUITING THE DECISION-MAKERS

The final piece of the jigsaw is what the key managers or departmental heads think. Inevitably they will think you want to discuss reward levels and budgets. However, this is the least of your worries. What you want from them is their general attitude to performance improvement and efficiency. Why? Because at the implementation stage you will need their active support in order to defend the concept, communicate the details to their staff and get the budgets approved. Performance improvement requires investment.

Each departmental manager will carry some mental baggage that needs to be understood and assimilated rather than criticised. The production director is keen to become more efficient but may be less interested in paying for it. The finance director will treat the problem of morale as mathematical rather than psychological. The sales director will already be looking forward to a trip abroad next year. The computer services director will not understand why there is any need to think about performance improvement at work at all, because in time we will all be working from home, won't we?

The attitudes of the more successful senior managers or directors need careful consideration. Several research studies that explored the prevalence of cash as a common motivator provided an unusual insight. Within business, successful executives tend to measure their own success in terms of personal wealth and luxury status symbols. This view is reinforced by the hierarchy above them which is constantly pushing for higher sales, lower costs and more profits; in other words, success is measured in money. When any performance improvement programme is discussed, there will be a tendency for senior people to consider that cash will fix the problem, in terms of higher rates of pay or target-driven bonuses. Research with middle level participants shows that above a basic comfort level, cash is less effective as a means of changing behaviour than non-cash rewards, or even simply peer or public recognition for a job well done. Money, after all, is only a symbol of worth.

So, you need to temper senior managers' views with an appreciation of their probable attitude to money as everyone's main motivator and steer away from instant solutions based on providing more cash. The process of performance improvement is far more complex than simply loosening the purse strings.

Agreement to a hypothetical budget is an important bridge to cross. You may be looking at somewhere between 5 and 10 per cent of total remuneration costs, post deductions, to make significant changes to behaviour. By anyone's standards that is a significant budget. Some companies work on a percentage turnover, anywhere between 3 and 5 per cent, if they are heavily sales led.

TAKING AN OVERALL VIEW

Once all the interviews have been written up, you need to take a sensible, middle of the road view. By exploring all these avenues, you should be able to propose a well-reasoned argument to invest in better human efficiency. With the initial audit complete, you can move on to developing the structure and rewards to suit your company profile and the current performance problems facing the company.

If you are a seasoned 'motivational interventionist' you may have already been through this initial research process, but you should avoid simply repeating the structure of an old programme, tempting as it is. There is still a need to examine whether last year's programme worked as well as it could.

We ran a programme for automotive aftersales people called The Gold Standard. In essence it was a glossy loose-leaf catalogue incentive, based on specific achievement of turnover against a target, with a few 'quality' tasks to underpin the performance. The message from the manufacturer was to emphasise the need to sell quality as well as sell volume. One without the other would be expensive in terms of poor repeat sales, so quality was crucial. As an investment, the programme returned about 20 per cent higher sales and a corresponding increase in quality. However, during the post-programme campaign analysis we researched in detail

Staff Incentives and Performance Management Techniques

attitudes to the campaign and asked for any improvements. There were a number of important comments ranging from encouraging more teamwork between different departments to specifying whether incentive tax was being paid for by the manufacturer and whether they could add cash to any awards claimed. It revealed that the length of the qualifying period for the programme was too short to make significant differences in ordering patterns for some suppliers. We were even able to float ideas about the appropriate type of rewards and structure for the next programme, so when it came to devising the follow-up scheme, the reward solution was already in the research.

TESTING YOUR PRESENTATION

If you do take the trouble to research the most recent programme, make sure you cover all the angles. The views of senior managers may not be the same as those of the staff or sales team. Communication of the detail may be clear to you if you have been living with it for the past three months, but it may not come across so clearly to junior secretarial staff or third party distributors who may only devote a fleeting few minutes to reading the brochure. It is well worth testing the understanding of the campaign mechanics before going live. We once ran a national quality standards programme for a major computer manufacturer, only to discover after the first phase that head office were the only section of the participants who understood what was on offer. We changed the design to be more pictorial and less wordy. The improvement in both understanding and acceptance was significant. Never underestimate the need to keep it simple, particularly with a disparate number of job types.

There are still no guarantees. A programme devised during boom-time is unlikely to work in the middle of a recession. If quality, defined as the predictable delivery of your product to a consistent standard, is your main failing, then a volume related sales incentive is a waste of money, not to mention time and effort.

The human audit is when all these things will be found out and provides a bedrock for future performance improvement.

Now you have a clear view of who you are trying to motivate, you can consider what techniques may be appropriate for your participants and how an effective programme could be constructed.

SUMMARY

- There are no instant solutions.
- Research each category in detail.
- Get the key decision-makers involved.
- Understand fully who does what, especially administrative staff.
- Talk to the 'old timers' about past schemes.
- Do specific research of the most recent initiatives.
- Check understanding of the communication materials.

3

CONSTRUCTING THE PROGRAMME

An axiom of virtually all the theories of motivation is that organisms strive to increase pleasure and to decrease pain.
Bernard Weiner

Scene: Top floor office suite of a multinational petrochemical company. Directors seated around a boardroom table.
Agency Account Director: In conclusion, what we propose is an integrated motivation programme, targeted to particular sub groups within the participant database, focusing on the need to appeal to both knowledge requirements and sales achievement. The result, if communicated to the degree we suggest, will enhance performance beyond the estimates laid down and produce incremental returns in excess of current expectations for the forthcoming financial year.
(Silence)
President: But where are we going?
Agency Account Director: Rio.

Most initiatives to construct a motivation programme start backwards. There is an urgency to develop the reward element in the hope that once the logistics of delivery have been arranged, performance improvement can take care of itself. In truth, sorting out the reward is the least troublesome of the tasks required to establish a profitable improvement programme. As in all marketing endeavours, establishing the objectives of the programme requires considerable thought if the expenditure is going to produce viable returns.

The human audit will have provided some clues as to the most pressing objectives, but now is the time to decide which course of action to take. This moment is usually a time of high anxiety as various departmental managers will all have differing views as to what to tackle first. Some will be more keen than others to press forward into action. The sales department may consider the task to be as simple as dangling a carrot in front of a donkey – and the bigger the carrot the better. Administrative supervisors worry about the precedent even a modest amount of discretional reward may set and whether the internal dissemination of performance achievement will be more divisive than beneficial.

At this point it may be useful to be aware of some important guidelines as to what works and what does not. A round-up of motivation theory may help.

MOTIVATION THEORY

Origins

The history of motivation theory only dates back as far as Freud and Jung. The first theories revolved around the hedonistic principle that what drives most people to act in a particular way is the pursuit of pleasure and the fear of pain. However, this truism was more of an observation about human nature than a principle which could scientifically predict what a given individual or group of people would do in specific circumstances. Clark Hull was the first to suggest some kind of general, predictive description of what motivates people. Based on the idea that behaviour is a function of an individual's inner drive and habit, he went on to establish that motivation is a function of drive, habit and incentive. Within a business context we recognise that some people appear to be 'well motivated' all the time, others require a pattern to follow (habit) in the form of working practices and standards to perform well. A significant group only perform well when there is something in it for them (incentive). Within the field of behavioural science Dawkins suggests innate selfishness is also a characteristic driving force of human behaviour. 'Our genes have survived in some cases for millions of years, in a highly competitive world. This enables us to expect certain qualities in genes. This gene selfishness will usually give rise to selfishness in individual behaviour.'

Atkinson was concerned with a theory of achievement motivation and suggested that people are driven to achieve by the conflicting tendencies to hope and fear. 'The possibility of success: the possibility of failure — the emotional conflict between hopes for success and fears of failure — individuals make a choice based on maximising personal hedonism.' In Atkinson's world achievement can be measured by calibrating the need to achieve, the probability of success and the value of the incentive being offered.

Henry Murray, in 1938, attempted to classify clinically what motivates people by categorising human behaviour into 20 basic human needs. One of them is the need to achieve:

> To accomplish something difficult. To master, to manipulate or organise physical objects, human beings or ideas. To do this as rapidly and independently as possible. To overcome obstacles and attain a high standard. To excel one's self. To rival and surpass others. To increase self-regard by the successful exercise of talent.

Other academics endeavoured to explain common observations of human behaviour. Cottrell in a study of social, interactive behaviours in 1972 pointed to improvement in performance when people act as a group. 'When two or more people act together, the intensity of their individual behaviour often increases.' Miller in 1959 proved clinically that 'the tendency to approach a goal is stronger the nearer the subject is to it'. McClelland tried to explain the rise of capitalism and entrepreneurial behaviour as a direct result of Protestantism — the reliance on individual effort rather than trust in the omnipotence of the Catholic church for guidelines on how to live in the second half of the 20th century. Fritz Heider suggested that all human behaviour depends on the social environment. 'When we say "he can do it", but fails only because he does not try sufficiently, then we mean that the effective personal force is smaller than the restraining environmental force ... with greater exertion he would succeed.'

Maslow's well-known theory of the hierarchy of needs goes a long way to explaining why offering higher level incentives (lavish holidays, peer group recognition) are ineffective if the basic needs of the individual to have food and shelter are not met. In other words high commission and low or non-existent basic pay or benefit is rarely the most effective way to motivate or retain people. Weiner summarised various experiments concerning expectancy levels of individuals in a given task-related situation: 'In skill related tasks, expectancies tend to increase after success and decrease after failure, pointing to importance of positive feedback when tasks are completed successfully.'

Recent developments

In 1992 Martin Ford put forward the most comprehensive review of motivation theory to date – the Motivation Systems Theory – which gives a dozen or so guidelines as to how to increase the likelihood of positive motivation. Put into a formula:

$$\text{Achievement (job competence)} = \frac{\text{Motivation} \times \text{Skill} \times \text{Responsive environment}}{\text{Biology}}$$

However it has to be recognised that all the academic work of the last hundred years has been sporadic in its usefulness within a business context. Many of the principles are either just plain common sense or simply not predictive enough to be sure-fire winners when it comes to developing the structure of a motivation programme. There is no magic, scientific formula for motivating people that will ring true in every conceivable situation.

That said, there are some general principles to bear in mind when planning the structure of a sound programme. By applying these principles you can lessen the possibility of failure and increase the effectiveness of your budget, but no set of principles can guarantee incremental profit. Experimentation and creativity will determine what works and what does not with a specific group of people.

Not every programme will require all of these principles, so slavish adherence to a formula will not guarantee success. You need to acquire a 'performance improvement mind-set' to guide all aspects of the programme from research to completion.

So, armed with the human audit, a brief historical perspective and some basic principles of motivation, where do you go from here?

PRINCIPLES OF CORPORATE MOTIVATION

- Motivation techniques need to be applied with a sensitivity to the corporate or social environment and any other factor peculiar to the individual or group. In broad terms you need to understand 'the big picture' before proposing solutions.
- To trigger performance improvement you need to combine a goal or objective, the subject's emotions and the subject's honest assessment that improvement is possible.
- The most important characteristic of a motivation programme is the setting of a relevant goal. If you are setting more than one goal, make sure they are not in conflict with each other. This is known as 'goal salience'.
- You must provide a method of feedback so participants can measure their performance and modify their behaviour.
- Be realistic about attainment standards and adjust them if participants are not achieving them. But continue to keep standards challenging.
- Use 'success stories' and peer group experiences to reinforce how individual performance can be improved and recognise successful performance.
- Provide skills training so that participants have the tools to achieve higher performance.
- Create an improvement process that is gradual and incremental rather than transformational. Complete change in one step is rarely greeted with enthusiasm.
- Try several overlapping techniques over a period of time. Don't expect one idea to work for everyone all the time. Create a developing motivation strategy.
- People are complex and unpredictable. Respond to feedback as quickly as possible, keep your promises and be interested in participants' reactions. A withdrawal of participant co-operation is a failure by the motivator to understand the process.

ISOLATING THE OBJECTIVES

One obvious starting point is what you hope to achieve by implementing the programme. In other words, decide on your objectives. Formulating a main objective and perhaps a few related subsidiary objectives is not easy. There are many interwoven business problems to be resolved during any given period. Like a doctor you need to separate the symptom from the disease, but if the human audit is sufficiently rigorous, you should be able to identify specific aims for groups.

Within a sales organisation, objectives come with the territory.

TYPICAL SALES TEAM OBJECTIVES

- Increase sales overall.
- Increase sales of specific products.
- Increase sales to particular clients.
- Increase sales through particular distribution systems.
- Increase sales in specific local regions.
- Increase sales of additional/complementary services.
- Introduce new products/services.
- Improve client retention.
- Improve repeat orders/new orders.
- Improve the level of average sales (quality).
- Run out old stock.
- Respond to competitor activity.
- Increase market share.
- Improve call rates and prospecting activity.
- Improve administration/paperwork.
- Improve salesforce retention.
- Improve team morale.
- Recruit new salespeople.
- Test product knowledge.

Almost all of these sales team objectives can combine with other objectives to a greater or lesser degree. Secondary objectives should not conflict with the main goal. For example, the introduction of a new product or service through a new distribution system should not coincide with a general drive on existing client retention or repeat orders.

In keeping with the principle of 'goal salience', it is more likely that the main objective will be more achievable if complementary secondary goals are promoted alongside. So, testing new product knowledge and introducing a new product go hand in hand.

Training

The importance of skills training cannot be over-emphasised in the quest to achieve lasting improvement. Incentives by themselves only produce short-term benefits. During the human audit process, training and skill development needs will be uncovered. Such issues need to be tackled if a long-term change is required. But it is not simply a question of booking people on a course.

Oldsmobile

The Oldsmobile Motor Division of General Motors was able to accelerate its ambition for higher customer satisfaction by personalising a skill development programme to each individual dealership. The process involved dealership employees completing a customer satisfaction survey from their customers' perspective. The results were then compared with the most recent customer satisfaction survey for that dealership.

The gaps provided the basis for three interactive customer satisfaction training modules over the following nine months. Success in the modules enabled the dealership to earn back part of the initial enrolment fee. All 65 of the original pilot dealerships increased their Customer Satisfaction Index. The system was then rolled out to the other 2900 dealers.

Measuring non-sales staff

Beyond the sales team arena, businesses often experience problems in defining measurable objectives, particularly if administration or line staff have never been measured before, except during formal appraisals. But non-sales people can be given objectives. The big debate is whether the cost of setting up and monitoring staff performance is worth the investment. In some cases it may not be.

TYPICAL STAFF OBJECTIVES

- Reduce absenteeism.
- Reduce costs.
- Invite ideas for higher efficiency.
- Promote teamwork and loyalty.
- Promote inter-departmental co-operation.
- Improve safety.
- Improve timekeeping.
- Increase productivity.
- Better staff retention.
- Improve quality of telephone contacts.
- Improve general communication skills.
- Monitor project progress.
- Check on morale.
- Check on training effectiveness.
- Improve budgetary control.
- Referral of sales opportunities.
- Recruitment of new staff.
- Direct sales (if applicable).

But with enough will to involve everyone in the organisation in performance improvement, much can be achieved.

But deciding the objectives is not enough. They must be measurable and have specific numbers attached to them, otherwise they become nothing more substantial than a wish list.

QUANTITATIVE OBJECTIVES

'To increase sales to clients by 20 per cent, by introducing new product Y and increasing orders retained by 5 per cent.'

Setting the quantitative figure needs to meet the criteria of reality. Has such a figure ever been achieved before? If not, what is so different about the new circumstances (apart from general optimism) to suggest you can achieve it this time? Are there any external factors in the market place such as legislation or the economy which may skew your quantifiable objective, either now or during the campaign? Will participants find the figure challenging but achievable? Or will they think you are just being far too hopeful? In a changing market where only you have access to positive trend research, but the general current mood is cautious, you need to share that research with participants so they can adjust their personal assessment of the future and change their behaviour accordingly.

For non-sales participants or support staff you can still quantify a remarkable number of so-called 'soft' tasks: the speed at which administration is completed; the quality of telephone contacts with internal and external customers; the reduction of accidents; the usage of stationery, photocopiers and the like; retention of staff. All these issues impinge on performance improvement in a highly measurable way and so can form part of an unequivocal programme in which everyone can take part.

In some cases, it may not be possible to allocate the necessary resources to track individual performance. This is particularly true within the multi-integrated activities of large listed companies. Although your ideal measurement may be to record all telephone calls during a programme and analyse their content, the incremental benefit may not be enough to cover the cost of the campaign.

Judgement by peers

We were once asked by a multinational IT company to devise a scheme to encourage performance improvement for all staff, including support and administration personnel. They had experienced sales incentives in the past but felt that directing the reward towards the front-line sellers alone did not truly reflect the team approach of a successful IT systems sale. We investigated all aspects of the process of the sale and discovered that virtually every support department was involved at some stage in the completion of the contract. But the cost of analysing job tasks, setting robust measures and monitoring support staff performance was far too great when compared with the likely incremental profit. The solution? We proposed the idea that the people who can judge your performance best are your peers.

So, why not get them to nominate colleagues who are perceived to have done a 'good job' over a given period? Guidelines were discussed to provide 'voters' with what the company would consider to be good performance. All nominations would then go forward, countersigned by the manager, to a national league. Those with the highest total were recognised publicly and rewarded appropriately. All awards were underpinned by each department/division having to achieve their profit target during the campaign period otherwise the reward would not be paid out. The programme has been running for 3 years and now operates across 12 European countries in several languages.

INCENTIVE TECHNIQUES FOR INDIVIDUAL PARTICIPANTS

Once the objectives have been decided, the next step is to find the right range of incentive techniques to deliver the best chance of a good result. Each element serves a specific purpose, but always check you have not cancelled out one element by introducing a complementary complication. The overriding factor should be to keep it simple. Imagine the participants reading the rules for the first time. Will they understand what is required? Will they understand the measure? Will they be able to plot their progress? Will they be able to change their behaviour? Will it be easy to participate?

1. Leaguing system

The most common mistake made in setting up a motivation programme structure is to base performance on absolute measures – top volume producer, highest team total, top national sales achievement. Every scheme needs winners, but if the winners can all be predicted at the beginning of the programme then you will fail to motivate anyone, beyond those who are already established as 'leading players'. Careful note should be made of what people will perceive as 'fair' (whether it is fair or not in reality is another matter). If everyone is ranked in order of absolute total volume, there will be few surprises at the end of the campaign and very little for those middle band achievers to aim for.

One simple way to create winners at many levels is to 'league' everyone. Within a sales environment this will involve putting similar achieving sales units together in a discrete league where they can compete with each other for the top awards.

Constructing the Programme

League examples
Problem: 100 dealerships, between £5m and £100m turnover
Solution: Create five leagues of differing sizes based on current turnover with awards for the top two in each league. Ten winners can be produced, thereby everyone has a 1 in 10 chance of winning rather than no chance at all below, say, the 30th ranked dealership.

One objection to this system may be that you are rewarding too many lower turnover dealers. You can tweak the structure according to your objectives by creating differing numbers of qualifiers per turnover league.

League 1	League 2	League 3
Dealer A	Dealer D	Dealer I
Dealer B	Dealer E	Dealer J
Dealer C	Dealer F	Dealer K
	Dealer G	Dealer L
	Dealer H	Dealer M
		Dealer N
		Dealer O
		Dealer P

In this way you can skew the chances of winning to those who produce habitually larger levels of turnover.

However, the middle band in any group of competitors often has the biggest capacity to improve (those ranked between 70th and 30th in a group of 100), so you may be wiser to consider how much more overall 'performance' you could get by giving the middle band the best chance of winning.

For example, you need to do your sums, but it is likely that a 10 per cent overall increase from leagues 2 and 3 would be worth more on the bottom-line than a similar level from leagues 1 and 2, because there are so many more middle band performers than top performers.

You do not necessarily need to publish how many competitors there are in each league to everyone in all leagues, if you think those with a lower chance of winning will feel discriminated against. As long as you tell those in any particular league how many places there are in their league, that is usually all they are interested in.

Within a staff environment, leaguing could be done by employee grade, job function or size of business unit. You may need to consider more creative criteria for placing people or groups of people in similar leagues. It could be number of transactions processed, the size of the local catchment area, rural or inner city, old or modern plant or equipment. Although the measures for staff usually need much more research and consideration to provide adequate checks and balances, making a staff scheme fair can be achieved with a little ingenuity.

2. Close-ended and open-ended

Structural choices often revolve around whether the competition should be open-ended or close-ended. In essence this means the difference between rewarding winners who achieve a personal target, regardless of other competitors' performance or having a specific number of winners, regardless of the individual's performance.

Close-ended schemes usually rank performance from top to bottom and offer, say, the top 10 per cent the 'big prize'. With 100 participants, there would be 10 winners, the top 10 only. This type of system is favoured where the company does not want to take the risk of over-achievement and having to provide expensive per head awards on the basis of freak market conditions or some unexpected loophole in the rules. In essence it is a defensive tactic from a diffident sponsor, who may long ago in the history of the company have got their fingers burnt. Motivationally it is less effective, but at least you have a fixed budget.

Open-ended schemes prove to be much more effective. People compete against their own target or a predetermined performance standard and feel more committed to a target which matches their situation. If they over-achieve, so much the better. Additional enhancements of the reward can be built in to encourage continuing improvement, once the target is reached.

Some careful analysis needs to be carried out prior to launch to agree a threshold that will be meaningful but challenging. In practice you may well predetermine that you wish to reward 20 per

Constructing the Programme

Table 3.1 The Advantages and Disadvantages of *Close-ended* Schemes

Advantages	Disadvantages
• Known budget • Specific number of winners • Rewards established participants • Easy to monitor/report • Top participants keep performing right up to the end of the campaign, if they are within the winning echelon	• Suggests company has a budget problem, ie does not want everyone to be a winner • Only motivates top echelon • Novices/middle band cannot win • Tends not to reward improvement • Winners can be predicted within a short space of time

cent of the participant universe; you look up last year's performance statistics and choose a threshold which will deliver rewards to all those in the top 20 per cent. You could argue that this is no different to setting up a close-ended scheme. The difference is that participants perceive the threshold to be a personal goal to aim for which they can plan to achieve. You cannot do anything about the performance of the other 19 in a closed scheme other than hope they fail. At least a specific threshold is an objective you can aim for without reference to other people. Competing with yourself is a powerful motivator.

Table 3.2 The Advantages and Disadvantages of *Open-ended* Schemes

Advantages	Disadvantages
• Participants compete against personal targets • Everyone feels they can win • Different targets can be set for different people in the same scheme • Scheme perceived as more equitable	• Cost not known until end of campaign • No single target suits everyone • Unusual market conditions can create too many/too few winners

Staff Incentives and Performance Management Techniques

There are many variations of open-ended and close-ended programmes to suit most requirements in any market situation. Work through the cost implications of various outcomes and test some likely result scenarios. There is the risk that your structure may reward the wrong people for the wrong type of performance, so it is vital to 'walk through' the process to see the likelihood of not achieving the objectives.

3. Commit-to-Win (sometimes called 'Bid and Make')

Participants declare in advance what performance increase they will attain (percentage improvement, specific threshold, number of tasks accomplished). The higher they aim, the higher the reward if successful. If they aim low and achieve high, rewards are less than if they had pitched high in the first place. The objective is to get sophisticated participants to bet against their own performance and aim higher than average. Experience shows that in overall terms more people achieve higher performance levels than they would otherwise do if given a set threshold. People are often surprised how much they can improve, given the right conditions. However, this option requires a certain amount of knowledge about personal past performance so that they can set challenging levels of future performance. Such a structure is unlikely to work if the participants are competing for the first time or are working with new performance standards.

4. Escalator

Points are awarded for achieving the threshold, with higher levels of points as each level is passed above that threshold.

Table 3.3 An escalator example

Level	Payment
Threshold	1000
110%	2000
120%	4000
130%	8000

Setting the points levels depends on being able to predict from past performance how many participants are likely to reach the upper levels. If you are thoroughly confident you may decide to 'escalate' ad infinitum, but most people set a cut-off level beyond which the points accumulated are fixed, or you risk being hostage to freak market conditions and bankrupting the company.

5. All or nothing

For those who like a challenge (and like to justify every penny to the financial department) one approach is to award nothing unless the threshold is achieved. Once it is, all performance points are retrospective. This enables you to set a challenging target (ie budget + 20 per cent), but promise a big reward in return. It has the major selling point of being simple to understand, but it does have one drawback. With no lower level rewards, average performers tend not to believe they can achieve the target and hence do not commit themselves as enthusiastically as you would like. Clearly, you need to have an understanding board if your team over-achieves against your expectations and you have a fixed budget. It is often the case that performance improvement funds are not flexible – they are usually part of a promotional budget based on sales or market share. With variations like 'All or Nothing' you can end up paying substantial rewards which will eat into other promotional areas if it is not carefully set up.

6. Sweepstake/lottery/raffle

The most unsatisfactory variation, but quite widespread in practice, is the sweepstake approach. Each percentage improvement or sale is worth one ticket in the 'reward sweepstake'. The more you improve or sell, the more chances you have of winning. This type of structure is mostly used by unsophisticated clients with an inadequate budget for the task in hand. By using clever promotion you can make the prize fund look very attractive. Although mathematically the higher achievers stand a better chance of winning the better rewards, it rarely works out like that in practice. More often a mediocre performer carries away the big prize by pure chance and feels embarrassed, while the higher level performers feel cheated and the sponsor (client company) is surprised it has left such a nasty taste. A refinement could be to restrict the 'chance' element to those who have attained a specific level, ie 120 per cent, thereby ensuring higher level performers will win the higher level prizes. There could be differing values of awards depending on the threshold they cross.

Promotional variations include scratchcards, sealed envelopes, lucky squares, lucky number phone-ins, matching cards, every fifth sale and a whole host of other devices to make the prize a secret until all is revealed. But it is still all based on chance and this is never a wholly satisfactory way to incentivise or reward performance improvement.

7. Fast starts, fast finishes

One of the problems with introducing any corporate initiative is the speed at which staff take up the challenge. The take up is normally very slow for a variety of reasons — inadequate launch communication, misunderstanding of the rules, too busy functionally to react quickly, an attitude of not-invented-here-so-I-will-not-cooperate.

One way to improve things is to build in an artificial accelerator at the beginning of the programme, normally known as a 'fast start'. This could involve extra credits in the opening period of the campaign to focus attention on getting the campaign introduced quickly and establishing the ground rules. An alternative could be to trade early achievement against a specific reduction in the end campaign target, thereby encouraging early performance. This is particularly suitable for new product introductions where speed of market penetration is essential.

Equally, the final period in any campaign may have specific significance for your market, but most well-constructed schemes do not have a 'fast finish' built in as the incentive itself is to achieve the standard before the end of the period. More typically a fast finish is introduced as an emergency measure to raise the profile of a mediocre campaign or to create more winners than would be expected, say, in a recessional period or following the unforeseen withdrawal of a specific product during the campaign which was beyond your control. (Double credits in the final month is a popular device.)

8. Weighting performance

One of the key principles in structuring a campaign is to achieve the participant's perception that the competitive element is fair. In other words, they all feel they can earn something at one level or another.

To achieve the perception of 'fairness', you need to consider a series of checks and balances so that participants do not immediately assess their chances of being successful as being nil. So, for distributors with differing turnover, you might adopt a league approach (see above). For staff in a sparsely populated area you may have to weight their volume of administration against a more busy city area so that comparisons are fair.

In some industries you may wish to remove certain products from the campaign, such as those which may sell at predictable levels anyway or may simply not be available on a national basis. Or you may wish to give 'customer service' twice as many credits as attendance, to emphasise its relative importance.

You may decide that you want to measure people by the amount of the improvement rather than the volume of activity. Measuring improvement against a personal benchmark is another way to equalise performance so that all participants feel they have an equal chance of success.

VARIATIONS FOR TEAM PARTICIPANTS

The variations in structure can be applied to teams as if they were individuals, except for one thing, namely peer group pressure. People working together exact considerable pressure on each other when they are aiming for a common objective. Depending on the degree of focus and leadership, the result can be better or worse than competing as individuals. You need to decide what best fits your corporate objectives.

1. **Total Team Performance** The team competes as if it were an individual and the rewards are equally distributed among the team, regardless of input, grade or experience.
2. **Points Pool** The team competes in the normal way, but the reward is divided up according to the contribution of each individual. This is relatively easy to define within a sales

environment and less so for administrative staff, but it does depend on the scheme. If staff are being objectively measured on such standards as absenteeism, timekeeping, attendance at training sessions, product knowledge and procedural accuracy, it is quite possible to reward according to individual performance as well as rewarding the whole team.
3. **Personal Bonus** The team could achieve a group standard for a specific team reward, with individuals receiving additional rewards for individual performance.
4. **Rank Order** Individuals within a team are rewarded in rank order of their individual performance.

Although throughout this book it has been argued that everyone in any job can be measured, the costs for measuring some types of employee can outweigh any incremental benefit, so rewarding the team may be best. However, it is even more important to ensure that the group task is clearly understood and that the challenge being set is perceived as fair. There will always be individuals who feel that they are unfairly targeted or that their local circumstances do not allow them to perform well. If this is the consensus view of a team, the value of the motivation scheme will be negative rather than positive. Individuals can be talked round to a positive view. Negative teams are hard work and you may find it less destructive to allow them to opt out rather than spread dissent. A vociferous number of isolated individuals is easier to handle than a vociferous team.

HOW LONG SHOULD THE INCENTIVE PROGRAMME LAST?

Some experienced sales directors never run any scheme longer than three months. Some human resources managers would not contemplate a performance improvement scheme which runs for less than a year. The answer lies somewhere in between and depends on the business objectives. There is no prescriptive answer for every situation, but experience suggests a few pointers.

1. **Standards Programmes** Where you are hoping to change working practices over the long term you will need to build in time for a pilot test and working roll out. Invariably business

Constructing the Programme

cycles need a year to work themselves through, so a general view would be an 18-month period, comprising 3 months' pilot, 3 months' assessment and amendments, and 12 months' initial programme.

2. **Tactical Sales Campaigns**   The length of tactical schemes is usually dictated by the call cycle of the industry or the length of the selling season. Anywhere between six weeks and three months is normal. A programme which lasts four weeks or less will rely heavily on very good launch communications within the network as even simple incentives take at least a week to get round even a modest size distribution chain. With short campaign periods it is difficult to influence a change of behaviour before the programme ends.

3. **Annual Programmes**   Where business is relatively predictable and not subject to fashion or consumer switching, annual programmes are more normal, tied into the financial reporting year. The structure could involve 2 or 3 tactical campaigns to coincide with known business peaks, and an overlaid scheme running for 12 months to incentivise and reward consistent performance over the year.

Although the marketing department may be aware when the tactical schemes will run, the participants will not, ensuring the company takes advantage of the element of surprise.

Within financial services a typical incentive programme might look like this.

Table 3.4 Annual Programme – tactical and strategic

Jan			
Feb		F	In this case, we have a 3-month
Mar		u	tactical campaign in the spring and a
April	Tactical	l	2-month campaign in early autumn,
May	Tactical	l	with an overlaid scheme for
June	Tactical		consistent performance running
July		Y	January to December
Aug		e	
Sept	Tactical	a	
Oct	Tactical	r	
Nov			
Dec			

51

Staff Incentives and Performance Management Techniques

Within the automotive industry, particularly in the UK, an alternative approach may be necessary to respond to market blips, combining car sales and aftersales (service, accessories).

Table 3.5 A Typical Incentive Programme for the Car Industry

	Cars	Aftersales
Jan	Tactical	Tactical
Feb	Tactical	Tactical
Mar	Tactical	
April		
May		
June		Tactical
July	Tactical	Tactical
Aug	Tactical	Tactical
Sept	Tactical	
Oct		
Nov		Tactical
Dec		Tactical

To incentivise showroom sales a first quarter campaign and a summer campaign may be appropriate. But this would be supported by a parallel scheme of tactical aftersales incentives to capture market share during the 'distress' winter period and the mid year days-out-with-the-family period. In the UK new cars are registered each August, so a volume incentive in the summer can pull through incremental sales.

4. **Riding the Peaks** People often debate whether tactical incentives should run during peaks or troughs in the revenue cycle. There is a natural reluctance to distribute rewards for sales which will largely happen anyway. Surely, we should be targeting the troughs to improve our spread and iron out the dips?

Each market is different but the most cost-effective schemes reap the most incremental performance when they are run during average months running into a peak or from a peak to an average period. Schemes run during troughs provide only a modest improvement and often prove to be an expensive way to buck the market. The explanation is logical. The reason for the trough is usually an unchanging market characteristic (ice-cream sells poorly in winter) which no amount of promotion will change. The principle is to boost sales in a favourable environment and try to prolong that peak as much as possible or until such time as the incremental returns are less than the investment.

RULES AND REGULATIONS

Whether for staff or salespeople, the rules and regulations of any performance improvement programme need careful thought for a variety of reasons.

1. Participants need to feel the way their performance will be judged is fair.
2. Participants need to know what will be included in terms of performance measures.
3. Participants need to know what the rewards will be.
4. Participants need to know about any hidden catches (tax liabilities, no alternatives to the stated awards).
5. The company needs to communicate clear parameters.
6. The company may need to exclude certain elements of performance.
7. The company may need to protect itself against deliberate misinterpretation by participants to gain additional rewards.
8. The company needs a written record of what was promised against specific criteria so that it can estimate its financial investment and liability.

If the rules are written by the financial director or consulting actuaries, it is likely you will never launch the programme, because there will always be some loophole, however unlikely, which cannot be closed by terms and conditions. The important thing is to keep the drafting of the rules in perspective and produce something which clearly states the way the programme works while protecting the company against inadvertent or mischievous misinterpretation.

For most campaigns, the rules need to follow these guidelines.

1. Who can participate?
2. Duration?
3. What rewards at what level?
4. Clarify any liabilities (tax, cost of travel to event)?
5. Arbitrator in case of dispute?
6. Communication policy during the campaign and at the end?

With complex programmes which may have four or five variants for different participant grades or types (sales, administration, plant, branches, distribution), you may need to produce a broad set of general rules for the glossy brochure and issue more detailed rules for each sub group of participants, depending on their involvement. But the golden rule is to ensure each participant has a copy of the rules relevant to their grade. Many companies make the mistake of only supplying the group manager with the rules. However adept a communicator that manager may be, they are unlikely to cover all the angles, resulting in some participants working to a performance standard which could actually have been excluded from the campaign. Full disclosure is the key.

SUMMARY

- Learn from the history of motivation theory.
- Apply the ten motivation theory principles, but only when appropriate.
- Isolate your objectives.
- Set quantifiable aims.
- Use appropriate incentive techniques.
- 'Walk through' the likely outcome.
- Check the rules for comprehensibility.

4

BUILDING THE BUDGET

I wouldn't invest in a business that didn't invest in its people.
Sir John Harvey-Jones

Once you have established who is to be included and which techniques to use, the next step is to propose a suitable budget. As large numbers of people are likely to be involved in the improvement process, any expenditure will be significant. A budget for motivation should be seen as a medium-term investment with a specific pay-back period. In most cases the budget will be self-liquidating. The only decision to make will be whether the company can afford to risk the initial set-up costs, because if a programme does not work, for whatever reason, the scheme will not produce any reward costs.

Setting a budget for a performance improvement programme is no different to setting any other budget for future expenditure. Certain assumptions need to be taken into account. However, many boards insist that incentive or performance programmes need to be 'self-funding' and seen to be so. The fact that the entire company is not self-funding until the report and accounts are filed at the year end is another issue.

No one can guarantee the future success of a performance improvement campaign. If they could, solutions could be logged and filed with a firm of reputable management consultants, and trotted out when the right conditions prevail. But there are ways to minimise the risk of failure. Many of those ways are described in this book. One further way is to draft up a sensible budget and make some reasoned, rather than simply hopeful, predictions of success.

THE CONCEPT OF INCREMENTAL PROFIT

Before you begin to add up all the expected costs, you should examine the overall objective: incremental profit.

All other things being equal, a well-planned incentive programme should produce additional turnover of between 10 and 20 per cent, sometimes more. Depending on your general view of the business climate, you can draw up an incremental profit objective.

Incremental profit example

Within the campaign period chosen, company A sells £1m of product. An incentive scheme is suggested to capitalise on an already successful period.

1. At 20 per cent additional sales, the campaign would provide £1.2m in revenue.
2. You know that additional revenue earns profits at 35 per cent margin (£70,000).
3. The company works on an allowance of 33 per cent to generate new business, so £23,331 will be available in the form of promotion and rewards.
4. If the fixed costs of launch and promotion are deemed to be an already-budgeted marketing cost, the actual money available for rewards would be £23,331.

The higher the margin – and it may be much higher if production set-up costs are ignored – the higher the amount available for rewards.

Summary

- Expected turnover without incentive £1m.
- Expected turnover with incentive £1.2m.
- Incremental revenue £200,000.
- Profit margin at 35 per cent = £70,000.
- Incentive budget at 33 per cent of profit margin = £23,310.

Setting the campaign target

The incentive budget of £23,301, represents 11.7 per cent (11.655 per cent) of additional sales. It would therefore be reasonable to suggest a campaign target of budget + 12 per cent (£1.12m). So, when the target is achieved, £23,310 will become retrospectively available for rewards and therefore the campaign becomes self-funding.

But, once turnover exceeds target, you can afford to be more generous with the rewards (see below).

Table 4.1 Campaign reward scenarios

Budget £1m	Target £1,120,000
1. **90% of target achieved** (£1,008,000 turnover)	• No rewards because target was not achieved. • As the budget was achieved, plus £8,000, set-up costs could be amortised.
2. **100% of target achieved** (£1,120,000 turnover)	• Rewards paid out at 33% of additional turnover; £40,000. • At 35% promotional margin, the company pockets £78,000 in incremental sales.
3. **110% of target achieved** (£1,243,200 turnover)	• Rewards paid out at 33% of additional turnover; £80,256. • At 35% promotional margin, the company pockets £158,080 in incremental sales.
4. **120% of target achieved** (£1,344,000 turnover)	• Rewards paid out at 33% of additional turnover; £114,552. • At 35% promotional margin, the company pockets £223,600 in incremental sales.

Provided the campaign target covers the original budget and the marginal cost of the rewards, a sales incentive can be self-funding.

COST HEADINGS

Once you have determined the incremental profit and therefore the campaign target, you need to consider what costs you are likely to incur. They will be either fixed or variable.

Fixed costs

- Initial roughs, research
- Creative concept fees
- Design for literature
- Artwork, film
- Copywriting
- Video scripting
- Video production
- Video copies, plus packaging
- Printed materials
- Collation, packaging
- Computer system set-up
- Distribution, launch postage
- Training manuals

It is difficult to be precise about costs, as much depends on the nature of the tasks to be completed. But in the unlikely event that the campaign has no effect whatsoever on performance, the initial fixed costs of between 10 and 12 per cent will not be recouped.

Variable administration costs

- Computer system administration
- Bulletin stationery
- Distribution of bulletins, other communication
- Reward based handling fees
- Selective training costs
- Agency consultancy, if applicable (10–15 per cent)
- Mid campaign research

Once the programme is in place, you can expect a further tranche of expenditure to ensure the administration and communication run smoothly.

Variable reward costs

This leaves an amount of between 73 and 80 per cent of the budget to cover reward and taxes. In the UK, assuming a grossed-up payment of 33 per cent for basic rate tax paid awards, the actual reward element comes to just 55 per cent of the total budget.

Table 4.2 Budget Summary Based on £100,000 Allowance

1.	Set-up and launch	£12,000
2.	Ongoing administration and fees	£15,000
3.	Rewards	£55,000
4.	Tax at 33 per cent	£18,315
		£100,315

From this example, particularly if tax is to be included, the sponsor needs to be aware that just over half the original budget will be set aside for rewards. With a salesforce of, say, 500, the initial calculation of 'What's in it for them?' on a per head basis of £200 has been whittled down to just £110 per head.

Clearly some savings can be made but each budget heading is there to serve a particular function. By diluting any element, you may be diluting the impact of the entire programme which will lead to less incremental sales and a hefty bill for set-up costs.

External set-up and handling fees paid to agencies are always negotiable, but you need to bear in mind that the lower the fees, the more likely it is that the agency will not be able to sustain as much account handling time as should be necessary, risking poor administration of the programme. Quality of administration is always worth paying for, whenever you are purchasing marketing services externally.

A word about agencies

Although formal non-cash incentive schemes and performance improvement programmes have been a feature of US business life for several decades, the concept of the 'full service motivation agency' is a relatively recent idea in the UK and Europe. My company conducted a UK survey in 1990 and established that over 70 per cent of performance improvement programmes were initiated by client companies, with many claiming no knowledge of specialist agencies in this field of marketing services. In fact most clients would turn to their advertising agency or sales promotion agency, before approaching a motivation agency. They would then front up any programme suggestion and subcontract the analysis and reward fulfilment to a variety of below-the-line suppliers.

The good news is that there are now a number of incentive and performance improvement specialists who operate ethical and reliable companies with enough clients to offer informed advice. But, as with most new areas of marketing services, it is worth while looking into the historical roots of the agency you appoint as those roots may well dictate the type of advice you are given.

Whatever the commercial title of the agency, most come from one of the six following marketing services backgrounds:

- merchandise;
- travel;
- sales promotion;
- training;
- event management;
- conference production.

Some have successfully integrated all their products into a completely rounded service, adding consultancy to create suitable solutions to performance improvement problems. Others have yet to leave their product roots behind and enjoy variable levels of success, depending on the brief.

As the Marquis de la Grange quipped most appropriately back in 1872: 'When we ask advice, we are usually looking for an accomplice.' Make sure your chosen agency has the strength in depth to give objective overall advice before investing the entire budget in the agency's favourite product.

If things change, so should the budget

Business has a habit of not coming in when you expect it in the mix you prefer. With long-term programmes there are many external influences which can affect the eventual cost of an incentive scheme.

If you spend too much proportionally on the initial launch and government legislation or a competitor makes your product obsolete, those fixed costs will be wasted. If you allocate too much credit to a particular product and freak marketing conditions make it the hottest thing since the invention of the frisbee, you may find yourself paying out thousands of pounds in reward to each individual rather than hundreds. If your company merges or is bought by another company, assumptions of who will sell what over a given period will now be somewhat different.

As long as you have set up targets based on incremental sales, the more the merrier. If not, you may have to go cap in hand back to the finance department who may tell you 'there is no more money', even though you can prove that more sales means more profit. An incremental budget for a subsidiary has a habit of becoming a fixed budget when the parent company has to approve the overspend.

SUMMARY

- The concept of incremental profit means most incentives should be self-funding.
- Campaign targets are different to budgets.
- Examine fixed costs and variable costs in detail.
- When taking external advice beware of being sold inappropriate reward media.
- Recalculate your budget if circumstances change.

5

CASH OR NON-CASH, THAT IS THE QUESTION

The fact that an opinion is widely held is no evidence whatsoever that it is not utterly absurd.

Bertrand Russell

Now that you have identified the business problem, and decided the strategy and structure of a performance improvement campaign, there are one or two ghosts to lay before you can begin to consider the reward elements. One is money, the other is employee benefits. Because offering cash is where most people start when it comes to thinking motivationally, we need to examine its efficiency.

Why not just give people more money? It is usually the first reason people give for leaving their current employment. It is the largest expenditure item in any company's overheads. In the UK, with a long tradition of industrial relations, monetary reward is something everyone can agree about, even if they have differing views about how much.

If in doubt, the pay plan can always be manipulated to suit the type of employee or third party seller. Assuming someone is getting the generally accepted 'going rate' for the job, you can cut the pay cake several different ways:

- basic salary, annual increments;
- commission for each item sold/sales achievement;
- performance related pay;

- stock options;
- other benefits.

Few companies offer just one of these elements in isolation. A combination of ways to be paid offers the opportunity to reward people on a short-term and a long-term basis, depending on the company's objectives and pay strategy for that particular group of employees.

BASIC SALARY

Providing the job description has been drafted correctly and some soundings taken of the local and national market for a particular job role, setting a salary provides the basis for rewarding long-term effort. The advantages to the employer are its administrative simplicity (the same amount each month), task orientation can be tied directly back to the job description and differentials in basic pay among the same job grade can reflect loyalty or competence.

However, as an aid to improving performance, it does very little. There is no incentive to try harder or make any extra effort, beyond the competitive pride or personal job satisfaction of the individual. Deviant behaviour such as absenteeism or deliberate non-cooperation does not usually result in a loss of earnings. Comparison with other employers is easily made, if there are no other incremental benefits within the pay plan, and so there may be difficult and expensive judgements to make at the end of each year at salary review. Because a salary is not usually contingent on job performance, companies which adopt the salary-only approach tend not to establish even basic performance criteria and measurement. This results in a minimum effort culture where the success of the business rests largely on product development and the economic climate. As Michael Le Boeuf, professor of management, University of New Orleans, points out: 'Reward people for the right behaviour and you get the right results. Fail to reward the right behaviour and you are likely to get the wrong results.'

By not rewarding risk takers, the company rewards precisely the behaviour syndrome it would rather not have.

For salespeople on a pure salary pay plan, it can lead to missed sales opportunities, loss of top sales employees tempted away by a competitor's bigger salary offer plus commission and the risk that in a cyclic downturn, the company may have far too many salespeople for the income they generate.

In practice there are few companies who offer just a salary so it may be more realistic to consider what performance improvement advantages there may be in combining salary with the various forms of performance related pay.

SALARY PLUS COMMISSION

A basic salary plus a commission for salespeople is the most popular way to encourage higher performance improvement. But you have to get the ratio right between salary and commission. If there is too much salary, people tend to perceive the commission as 'fun' money and so it becomes less effective as a driving force. If the commission element is too great, people start to cut corners on quality of service and business ethics to ensure they can at least meet their minimal monthly outgoing commitments.

The general guideline is that anywhere between 15 and 35 per cent represents an effective ratio for commission compared with basic salary, depending on the market sector.

However, the commissionable element of any remuneration plan requires sound administration and a thorough understanding of the 'rules of engagement' when deciding what to award. In many industries it is becoming harder and harder to attribute particular sales or contracts to single individuals. Even the archetypal salesperson − the life assurance seller − is often supported by technical specialists who assist the sale in complex cases.

For large contract sales, where a relationship has been built up over the years with a succession of representatives, a tender document is normally produced with the assistance of a team of technical staff. It may be the financial director, in the final analysis, who decides what fee to charge, thereby positioning the bid that wins the contract. Should the last salesperson in get the commission? Should the support team receive any? Should everyone in the company benefit directly?

But perhaps the most difficult aspect of running an effective commission system is defining who made the sale.

> **DEFINING THE SALE**
>
> - Initial desk research into the opportunity (identifying the prospect).
> - Initial telephone call.
> - Initial letter (not acknowledged).
> - Initial letter (acknowledged).
> - Voice contact, in person or by phone.
> - Credentials presentation.
> - Meeting to discuss the specific project.
> - Presentation of the response.

All of these stages in the sale could be deemed to be the crucial moment when the potential client became aware of the potential supplier. But in a mature market where the main players for a particular service or product are known, an incoming contact from the client by letter or telephone could spark off the start of a sales relationship. In such a situation should the salesperson who simply picked up the phone receive commission? If so, should it be the same level of commission as if the salesperson had researched the client over two years before finally clinching the deal?

Crediting sales to individuals becomes even more complicated when a company has an existing client bank with many divisions to sell into. Is it still a sale to sell the same thing to the same client two years running? Or, worse still, should commission be paid to a salesperson for a sale which is a repeat order when the salesperson has not been in contact with the client for two or three years, other than reading reports from the technical team?

If commission levels were minimal, the question of credit is less important, but with levels of 25 to 30 per cent, significant sums are involved which can cause considerable demotivation of support staff, particularly if they know the salesperson made no contribution at all to the repeat sale.

Prospecting – rewarding the process

Depending on your business strategy for acquiring new business, you will lend more or less importance to specific prospect-related achievements. You need to find the balance which suits your objectives and culture and write the rules accordingly.

Table 5.1 The Prospecting Reward Process

Activity	Performance Improvement Strategy
Identifying the prospect	Reward the number of prospects
Initial telephone call	Reward the accuracy of prospect data
Initial letter/follow-up	Reward the ratio of positive responses to letters sent
Voice contact	Reward ratio of calls to prospect voice contact
Credentials	Reward number of credentials made
Briefing meeting	Reward ratio of briefs received to credentials made
Actual sales	Reward ratio of sales to initial telephone call

Within large corporations that may span several industries, you will need to define whether direct sales made in one division should be credited to a salesperson who has a relationship with a totally separate division, but who has no contact with the first division.

A good strategy is to draw up a list of well-defined rules so that there is no doubt about when credit is due so that individual claims do not have to go for 'adjudication', wasting valuable management time and not furthering the business process in any way. You need to consider all the possible anomalies so that the system is clearly understood by those who are participating and those who may be responsible for calculating how much commission is due.

Commission has been the mainstay for many organisations relying on rapid penetration and distribution within large markets. In some consumer markets where sales depend on aggressive personal marketing (automotive, insurance, high value home improvements) commission is effective in promoting high energy levels, and fast growth in turnover and wide product distribution.

However, the higher the value of the item, the more likely that mis-selling will be subject to legal regulation or trade ethics, resulting in commission disputes or worse still deliberate

Staff Incentives and Performance Management Techniques

TYPICAL COMMISSION RULES

1. Commission will be payable on all sales between 1 January and 31 December.
2. A 'sale' is defined as a signed contract from the client.
3. New client sales are defined as:
   - new sales from new clients;
   - new sales from new divisions or subsidiaries of existing clients;
   - new product sales to existing clients.

   A rate of X per cent will be paid for new sales.
4. Existing client sales are defined as repeat orders from existing clients. A rate of Y per cent will be paid for existing client repeat orders.
5. To claim commission the seller needs to attach supporting documentation (telesales report, letters sent, letters received etc) to establish that, without the seller's intervention, the sale would not have happened.
6. The amount of the claim should be based on invoiced items, less purchase tax and any discounts granted.
7. Resignation will result in loss of commission for items invoiced after the letter of resignation is received.
8. Commission will be capped at £50,000 for any individual client (or other relevant upper threshold).
9. Claims will be subject to quality audit and may be denied if minimum operating standards are not met.

inappropriate selling which tarnishes the entire market sector and the image of the company.

With growing consumerism and a reduction in the cost-effectiveness of 'selling direct' excessive commission as a viable way to promote higher performance will become less defensible. Consumers will demand more service-orientated marketing.

PERFORMANCE RELATED PAY (PRP)

Linking pay to performance is not the prerogative of sales or customer facing staff. In July 1991 the Citizen's Charter in the UK stated that there should be a 'regular and direct link between remuneration and standards of service'. This statement is really a description of what most companies had been moving towards since the mid 1970s. The argument goes that people will be more motivated if their remuneration is linked in some ways to their performance (just like the traditional salespeople).

A proliferation of ways to achieve this sprang up: profit share; team pay; share ownership/options; gainsharing; profit related pay; skill and competence pay; merit pay etc.

Some schemes offer tax-free income for compliance with specific Inland Revenue regulations. Others are devised by the sponsoring company to kick in when a certain level of company profit before tax is achieved or a predetermined operating standard is attained. Some companies have used the concept as a means to break the annual cycle of expectation where employees receive an annual increment with an extra bit for merit, if the company can afford it. It can mean no annual increment. Increases are determined by company performance against budget or market share.

Provided the parameters are clearly set out and participating individuals understand how they can influence the result, PRP can be an effective way to communicate the message that everyone can contribute to the greater good.

Disadvantages of PRP

However, this is rarely the case. Schemes triggered by residual profit often fall flat because the means to effect the profit equation (fewer overheads/more revenue) are not easily able to be calculated and communicated except at the year end. Within large corporations, profit levels may depend more on inter-group charges or local subsidies than any cost-cutting or efficiencies the employees may undertake. If you cannot as an individual see how your personal performance can make a difference, you are unlikely to change your behaviour. You are certainly not going to change the way you work for less than a 5 per cent take-home bonus.

In addition such schemes tend to attract arcane methods of calculation known only to the finance department and the amount of profit share available is as much a surprise to the company directors as it is to the mail room. The extra money is duly pocketed some months after the end of the year (official audits need to be carried out to verify the final, year end figures), by which time no one can remember what behaviour they are being rewarded for. The bonus becomes a post-dated reward rather than a dynamic incentive to promote performance improvement.

By their very nature such schemes tend to produce a relatively low reward as a percentage of salary (less than 5 per cent) which is not enough to promote a change in behaviour for the following year from most individuals. Various studies suggest that at least 10 per cent of take-home pay is necessary to activate a fundamental change of behaviour, particularly among middle management salaried staff who have reached their 'comfort level'.

MONEY – THE WORST MOTIVATOR

So, why do we use 'more money' so often as an incentive only to be disappointed by its lacklustre effect?

When you ask individuals in organisations the basic question as to which type of reward would motivate them to work harder, the top answer is always more money.

Table 5.2 Reward Media – Percentage of Companies Using Them

Reward Media	Per Cent
Cash	43
Overseas travel	35
Vouchers	23
Merchandise	20
UK breaks	16
Sports events	14

Source: Page & Moy Marketing Ltd

Cash, whether as salary, commission or some form of PRP, does have its merits. If you want to find out more, *Reward Management* by Michael Armstrong and Helen Murlis (Kogan Page) surveys all the current options and structures of devising pay plans.

However, as a means to encourage performance improvement

cash does have severe limitations. One of the most telling research findings about PRP comes from a study by Jenson and Murphy, University of Rochester, cited by US *Business Week* in 1987, in which they compared the relationship between pay and overall corporate performance. After analysing the performance of 2000 executives across 1200 different companies in the US they concluded there was no real correlation between PRP and company performance, and what's more, 'executives tend to be overpaid for bad performance and underpaid for good performance'.

A follow-up study in 1989 by Berlet and Cravens covering 163 US companies also concluded that the link between executive performance related pay and a company's performance was virtually random.

An Institute of Manpower study in 1993 in the UK also found that performance related pay *by itself* not only failed to improve staff performance but actually led to a 'downward spiral of demotivation', if customer demand was poor. A general view that whatever effort you put in could not change a flat market into a buoyant market was commonly held.

There comes a point when all managements ask the same question. Why doesn't throwing more money at performance problems work, especially when even the staff say that more money is what they want? Beyond the employees' comfort zone how can a manager motivate staff to make that extra effort? Why does cash seem to exhibit ever-diminishing returns?

Victor Vroom: Work and Motivation, 1964

One of the seminal experts on the effect of cash was Victor Vroom. He discovered that once a specific comfort level had been reached, offering more money in return for improved performance actually impaired performance as it created unproductive stress. It reinforced the view of the workforce that management can only think of staff as economic units, to be manipulated like plant and machinery to create higher profits.

Management teams which were perceived to motivate purely with money formulae were perceived as cynical and uncaring. By setting ever-increasing performance criteria linked solely to ever-higher cash amounts, employers created high levels of stress and anxiety to the point that some individuals refused to participate any further and withdrew their, until that point, willing co-operation.

A self-fulfilling prophecy

The preponderance of cash as a motivator is so widespread in Western industrialised society that it begs the deeper question as to why it is used so often if it actually creates diminishing returns.

As already suggested in Chapter 2, those who rise to positions of power tend to value money as the most important measure of worth and efficiency, particularly in entrepreneurial companies – a theory developed through several studies about the motivational effect of money. This leads to a propensity to use cash as a means to reward higher performance rather than other managerial techniques or non-cash rewards. Research carried out by Professor E R White shows that the psychological profile of successful entrepreneurs tends to perpetuate the idea that money or its accumulation is everyone's major driving force. More money becomes a self-fulfilling prophecy as a means to motivating people. If it works for me, the boss, it should work for everyone else, shouldn't it?

In other words, people have been subjected to extra cash for so long and so often as an incentive that participants feel it must be what they want, otherwise why would it be offered so relentlessly in their working lives, whatever their job?

Trophy value

An aspect of money as a poor motivator is its inherent lack of image. It has no 'trophy' value. People do not like to talk about how much extra money they have earned in a given period to friends and relatives, although they will talk about being given a letter of commendation or being taken out to dinner by the boss or an invitation to a prestigious overseas travel event, or some other non-cash privilege. It is simply not socially acceptable to boast openly about how much you earned last month. Also, money tends to be absorbed into everyday expenses and once paid electronically into the bank merges with the rest of the monthly income. Its use as a reminder of a job well done is soon forgotten, both for employee and employer.

As society in general becomes more affluent, most people in employment are not living on or below the poverty line. Most people are able to generate slightly more income over their regular expenditure beyond pure subsistence, so additional cash income is less of a powerful motivator to change behaviour. People have achieved a comfort zone to the extent that the extra effort to accumulate more money is not worth the incremental pain of achieving it.

Cash is expensive

In the UK, cash is also more expensive as a reward or incentive medium than non-cash. Under the UK's fiscal regime (1995) cash is 18 per cent more expensive than non-cash for the company to supply. A combination of employers' National Insurance, the time lag before personal income tax is due and the discount normally available for non-cash items results in substantial employer savings, by avoiding cash altogether.

Table 5.3 What Cash Costs the Company

Cost Differential on £100	Cash	Non-cash
● Original award	£100	£100
● Employer's National Insurance 10.45%	£13.90	Nil
● Tax at 33%	£33.33	£33.33
● Interest cost due to delay in tax liability	£4	Nil
● Market discount (5%)	Nil	Nil
Total Cost to Employer	£151.23	£128.33

As for the participant, if the employee opted for a cash payment rather than a non-cash payment, the difference in 'income' is due to the differing fiscal treatment of National Insurance on cash and non-cash.

Table 5.4 What the Participant Takes Home

Income Differential on £100	Cash	Non-cash
● Amount	£100.00	£100.00
● National Insurance	less £13.93	less £3.48
● Balance	£86.07	£96.52

So, not only does the company pay more if it opts to reward with cash, also the individual receives less if they are rewarded with cash. It all adds up to a bad deal.

In summary, these are the disadvantages of cash:

- It is more expensive than non-cash.
- It has little trophy value or memorability for recipients.
- It suggests the company is cynical and manipulative (and devoid of imagination).
- It is an easy, but ineffective option, especially for employees in the comfort zone.

But if you are stuck with a cash incentive scheme for whatever reason, you can still make more of it if you have to use cash as a motivational lever despite the inherent disadvantages.

A national parcels and documents delivery company had been running a monthly cash bonus for its workforce for many years. Each month in the pay slips, employees would receive a definitive amount of extra money (£86.25, £14.34, £120.78) for 'performance'. Unfortunately, no one, except the financial director, knew what the performance criteria were. So, the original objective to improve performance quickly became a retrospective reward for historical achievements which remained largely mysterious. This was a classic case of an innovative idea strangled by the payment process.

What they needed to do was communicate with the workforce how the monthly sum was calculated and explain what the performance measures were so that participants could at least try to match last month's performance, if not better it.

It transpired during the research phase that the formula for payment was based on divisional profitability factored by current salary. As a system it certainly ensured that rewards were linked directly to profits, but there was no link to the everyday working practices of the employees.

A long hard look was taken at what people actually did and what constituted 'good performance'. Delivery drivers, for example, were asked how they thought their performance might be best measured. They suggested such elements as timekeeping, getting legible acceptance signatures from clients, delivering jobs on time, planning the call cycle, asking for additional orders. This process continued with the clerical staff and the salesforce. At the end of the investigation period it proved relatively simple to devise a communication programme for each individual showing their personal performance against their key tasks and hence their cash bonus level.

Money is not the answer

The advice is clearly not to outlaw money completely as a motivator. That would be nonsense. But it has to be put in its rightful place if the discussion is about effective incentives. Money will certainly reward people for an historic job done well (or even adequately), but in isolation it rarely works as well if you are looking for improved or incremental performance.

SUMMARY

- Salary, commission and PRP have their place in rewarding historic performance.
- But cash costs 18 per cent more to provide than non-cash.
- Beyond an employee's comfort zone, cash exhibits diminishing returns.
- More money is the least efficient and effective motivator.

6

FLEXIBLE BENEFITS

> The chief value of money is that one lives in a world in which it is over estimated.
>
> **H L Mencken**

You are now armed with an understanding of motivation techniques and have considered the merits or otherwise of cash *v* non-cash, but you still have one corporate financial hurdle to clear before you can start to use non-cash rewards.

What about the 30 per cent or more of the annual salary bill paid out in benefits of various kinds, from life assurance to child care vouchers? Surely this represents a major opportunity to promote performance improvement using a financial commitment which already exists? But the problem is that few employers know exactly who is getting what at any moment in time, especially in larger companies where details of individual benefits may be held by different departments in a variety of formats. For benefits to be used as a performance incentive or loyalty reward, the employer needs to get a clear view of who is receiving what amount of benefit on an individual basis, otherwise how can you set any form of individual benchmark? But, how effective is this spend and does it motivate people to work harder or stay in a job for longer than they otherwise would?

Benefits do not fall neatly into Herzberg's theory of motivation factors. Benefits can be satisfiers or dissatisfiers. Depending on how the benefits are communicated, the employer could be either wasting the investment or reaping a huge improvement bonus. The key factor is whether employees perceive their benefits as valuable or simply part of their rightful remuneration. Are benefits as elusive as cash when it comes to their motivational potential?

The first questions to ask are what are employment benefits and why is there a mood of change sweeping through the advanced industrialised nations to reappraise the value of benefits as part of a total remuneration package?

BENEFITS AS SECURITY

In the last three generations, the world has experienced two global wars, nuclear physics, the establishment and collapse of Soviet Communism, and varying degrees of individual freedom within an increasingly industrialised society. These factors have conspired to produce a general acceptance that the employer as well as the state has a duty to provide a certain degree of financial security and stability. In some companies in the late 19th century this manifested itself in worker communities set up and regulated by the company to ensure loyalty and a reliable source of labour. By cocooning the employee in subsidised housing, offering social facilities and providing other supportive systems, employees began to expect that the employer should take on a paternal as well as an economic role, rather like a Victorian patriarch; strict but fair. Those employers who did not were perceived as old fashioned and exploitative. So strong was the pressure that eventually legislation ensured that some employment benefits became statutory rather than optional. The concept of the 'nanny state' was born.

Clearly, within the context of social history this was a good idea; less worker exploitation, higher living standards, more job stability, and competition between employers to deliver a bigger and better remuneration package to attract skilled and semi-skilled employees alike.

But times change. Although many employees now enjoy a range of benefits never dreamed of by their grandparents, questions are being asked about whether today's employees really appreciate their value. Western employers are asking whether such benefits can be justified in a global market where many Third World suppliers do not as yet carry the heavy burden of all this accumulated expectation of employee benefits. Younger employees are also questioning the relevance of such benefits as pension contributions and life assurance when they have only a vague appreciation of their ultimate value.

BENEFITS AS LOYALTY INCENTIVES

A solution seems to be presenting itself. Why not give people benefits which match their individual situation? The answer is flexible benefits or 'flex plans', as they are known in the US.

Born in the US from the need to control the spiralling cost of health care, US employers began to offer flex as a means of reducing overall cost exposure. In the late 1980s Chrysler calculated that up to US$800 per car went on employee benefits. Something had to be done to reduce this increasing cost problem. In Western Europe, most companies offer a limited range of financial products designed to cater for major life events: life assurance; pensions; sickness or disability benefit. In the US, Canada, South Africa and more recently Australia, the concept has been expanded to include a whole range of benefits in the drive to give employers more control of company expenditure, and the employee more choice and value for money, with a possible spin-off, in terms of recruitment and loyalty.

Table 6.1 What is Meant by Benefits?

Money	Health/Family	Insurance	Other
Salary	Health screening	Life assurance	Mobile phone
Share/stock options	Dental care	Pension	Home computer
	Eye care	Disability insurance	Car
Credit car subscriptions	Counselling (legal/personal)	Critical illness cover	Car parking
		Accident cover	Private fuel
Interest on loans	Creche	Short-term sick pay	Non-vocational training
	School fees	Household insurance	
Short-term savings plan	Child care vouchers	Motor insurance	Luncheon vouchers
Housing subsidy	Elderly parent support		Subsidised restaurant
Financial planning	Sports and social facilities		Relocation
			Holidays

It is clear from this list that individuals will want different types of benefit at varying levels. The tax regime in each country may also determine which benefits represent good value.

You can imagine what benefits individuals might prefer, depending on their personal circumstances. But it is difficult and dangerous to predict what employees want without full consultation. Every workforce is different.

However, there are some common main drivers for employees when it comes to benefit choice, although most choices reflect what is uppermost in the minds of employees when the choice is offered.

DRIVERS OF BENEFIT CHOICE

- More time off.
- Loss of health.
- Making ends meet (more cash).
- Flexibility if circumstances change.
- Value for money.
- Security.
- Prospects of advancement.
- Status (both perceived and actual).

The important thing is to ask employees what they would prefer, given the choice, although some care should be taken in the research process not to set up expectations that cannot be delivered when the new scheme is launched.

Employee types

All employees are not the same, as the following examples show. But even those listed below are stereotypes and may not match your own workforce profile. Indeed, one employee's ideal benefits package may not meet the needs of another employee, who may be at the same grade doing the same job.

1. SINGLE, UNDER 30 YEARS OLD

- Disposable income.
- Disability insurance.
- Extra curricular training.
- Meal subsidies.
- Sports facilities.
- Mobile phone.
- Car.

2. MARRIED WOMAN WITH YOUNG CHILDREN: WORKING PART-TIME

- Sick pay.
- Life assurance.
- Child care vouchers.
- Holidays.
- Health screening.
- Housing subsidy.
- Medical insurance.
- Creche.

Staff Incentives and Performance Management Techniques

---

3. MARRIED MAN, 45 YEARS OLD: MAIN FAMILY BREADWINNER

- Life assurance.
- Pension.
- Disability insurance.
- Eye care.
- Dental care.
- Housing subsidy.
- Credit card subscriptions.
- Car.

These deliberate caricatures illustrate the advantage of flexible benefits. Each individual is given, as part of his or her remuneration package, a specific number of 'credits' which can be spent, to varying degrees, on any or all the benefits on offer, or indeed be converted into cash. Many benefits will depend on the value for money as perceived by the employee as to whether they will be more or less prized as part of remuneration. But the principle is sound: free choice, according to your personal circumstances. Because there can be significant cost savings in buying some benefits in bulk or because the employer feels a moral obligation to protect employees in cases of hardship (life assurance, health care), many schemes include a number of 'core' benefits which everyone receives up to a minimum level.

Defined costs

There is a significant advantage to the employer here and that is cost control. In other words, employers can move to a 'defined cost' for benefits rather than the open-ended cost so characteristic of many current non-flex benefit schemes. For the employee it is value for money. Perhaps for the first time, by going through the process of creating a flex plan, the employer will have identified what benefits are valued by each individual employee. It can represent a finite cost within the company budget but as most benefits are individually costed, there will be different benchmark figures for each age group or business unit. When new recruits are taken on or package negotiations are taking place with more senior level appointments, there is no longer any need to horse-trade on various benefits. The package could include 30 per cent or more 'in benefits'. Negotiation can be about the percentage range, but there is no need to wonder whether offering a better car or a bigger pension allocation will do the trick or be in conflict with peer group employees. That decision is left to the employee. It removes all the status anomalies so prevalent when you compare senior management packages even within specific industries and allows the human resources department to budget their spend more accurately. In the UK market, where benefits for senior appointments could be over 50 per cent of salary, more accuracy on expenditure is a welcome tool for sound management of overheads.

In the UK in the 1990s there has been much more openness about executive remuneration. Such initiatives as the Greenbury Report on executive pay and the Nolan Report are leading to more and more transparency concerning benefits, and this will eventually feed into more communication when it comes to what less senior employees receive as remuneration. People want to know more about the actual cost of benefits and demand is growing from the workforce to choose the benefits that suit them.

So much for theory, what about the practice?

Some very big companies have already gone the flexible benefits route: PepsiCo Foods International; Mercury Communications; Colgate Palmolive; Saatchi & Saatchi; Royal Mail; CIGNA. But not all of them have included every employee in their schemes. Each company had its own cultural problems to overcome. All realised that sound advice, good internal communication and administrative excellence are required to introduce the change successfully.

Key stages of 'flexing'

There are some key practical issues to bear in mind before becoming a born again 'flexer'. There are many unforeseen variables which need careful consideration before overhauling such a high overhead. Getting it wrong could mean the company risks raising expectations it cannot deliver, making it impossible to raise the flexible benefits issue in the future.

PRACTICAL POINTS

- Pinpoint the strategic reasons for switching to a flex plan.
- Study competitor activity.
- Get commitment from senior management and unions.
- Start the dialogue with providers.
- Consult with employees.
- Build and test a working model.
- Communicate with employees.
- Examine the tax and insurance issues carefully.
- Plan for additional administration.
- Amend in the light of experience.

Probably most important of all, get professional advice to guide you through these stages, even if you decide to do most of the research and development yourself.

Flexing for the right reasons

Many accountancy-based management consultancies will argue that flex plans can deliver increased staff retention and therefore lower recruitment costs in the future. This has never been proved although the argument is a compelling one. Being more competitive when it comes to establishing remuneration benchmarks is certainly one of the bonuses of a flex plan, but there are more important things at stake. It is better to view things, at least initially, from a more strategic viewpoint.

A flex plan needs to be consistent with your company's strategic aims. If part of your strategy for personnel includes more empowerment, reducing layers of management, creating a flatter structure or simply responding to company cultural changes demanding more individual choice, then a flex plan could be part of the answer.

If you have a diverse workforce which typically includes a number of 'time-servers' as well as self-motivated high flyers, then a flex plan provides the opportunity to meet the needs of both groups in a single scheme.

If you are a modern, hi-tech employer which prides itself on creativity, innovation, team spirit and being seen to reward loyalty, a flex plan is one way to express this philosophy. If you genuinely feel that 30 per cent or more of your personnel overheads could be better utilised as a business investment by offering a personal choice of benefits rather than a standard package, then a flex plan provides distinct advantages.

But if your main aim is to reduce immediately the level of benefits you feel obliged to provide as a percentage of your overheads, because you want to raise profitability, then flex is not the answer. If you have an ageing workforce in a mature industry and want to avoid expensive final salary pension pay-offs, you would be better advised to talk to a pensions specialist, rather than expect a flex plan to deliver lower costs. If you think you already know what is best for your workforce in terms of benefits, then a flex plan will offer you no advantages.

Flex plans are about corporate personnel strategy and assessing the motivational value of benefits rather than a quick fix to avoid future liabilities or reduce current costs.

Once the board, with its advisers, has decided that a flex plan could deliver relevant advantages and is consistent with the company's personnel strategy, the next step is consultation with your employees.

THE CONSULTATION PROCESS

When you talk to professional advisers who offer flex plan consultancy, they all agree on the need to plan the consultation process carefully and never assume anything, however tempting it may be. Companies are typically atypical.

Mercury Communications

Russ Watling, human resources manager at Mercury Communications, the UK telecommunications company, suggests that the communication strategy of implementing their flex plan was crucial in its successful introduction and in gathering intelligence about how they could improve the way they get the message across to future employees. The Mercury scheme is the largest flex plan in the UK, involving over 10,000 employees.

The standard Mercury benefits package for all employees on permanent contracts includes 25 days annual leave, free private medical insurance, an employee assistance programme (EAP), a save-as-you-earn share scheme offering Cable & Wireless shares, an employee bonus scheme, discounted telephone and personal insurance products, and a competitive final salary pension scheme. The company spends over £50 million per annum on employment benefits in order to attract and retain the calibre of employee necessary to support the strategic goals of the business. It was felt that further improvements could be made to this benefit programme: first by making employees aware of how much the company was spending on their behalf (a fact which is often not brought to employees' attention); and secondly by introducing an element of choice to the benefits programme.

The Mercury workforce, like many, reflects a considerable social range and it was felt that the benefits programme was the one key feature of the employment process that did not include provision for the individual. For example, the appraisal, career development, training and remuneration policies all include the individual as a key factor, but the benefits programme tends to assume that everyone is the same. Flexible benefits were therefore developed to address these issues.

An internal feasibility study was started in December 1992 looking at the actual cost of benefits provision take-up, opportunities for flexing, which employees should be covered, tax, systems and pricing issues. A desk study of newly introduced UK flex schemes was carried out, and four companies agreed to participate in the research and provide information during interviews. A number of senior Mercury managers were interviewed about flex and the results were very positive. The Mercury board approved the provisional flex plan in April 1993.

Because the Mercury flex programme is on a comparatively large scale it was decided to introduce the idea to a pilot group of employees in advance of the main launch. This was done not only to test out the administration, systems and communications aspects, but also because the employees had not been consulted and this would enable feedback before the main launch. Flex was introduced to a pilot group of 400 employees in May 1993, principally in the research and development area. The programme was positioned as additional to the existing benefit entitlements and employees were able to choose whether or not they wished to take part. The response was very positive; 34 per cent of employees chose to vary their benefit provision and the general reaction was encouraging.

The benefits positioned within the flex programme are pension, life cover, health care, annual leave, dental insurance, car and child care. Not all of these were available for the pilot group but have been introduced since. All flex options are designed to be cost neutral to Mercury. Employees decide if they want to have the options and must commit to receiving their choice for a 12-month period.

Pension Employees in the pension scheme accrue retirement pension at the rate of 60ths for each year of service. This costs the employee 5 per cent of pensionable salary. Flex offers four new options where employees are able to trade up in order to accrue pension at a faster rate and either plan for early retirement or improve their existing pension potential. These are 55ths, 50ths, 45ths and 40ths. Employees can contribute up to a total of 15 per cent of salary, depending on factors such as how much they can afford, their age and past pension provision. The pension choices proved popular for the employees in the pilot group; 10 per cent of employees bought better pension cover.

Life cover Employees in the pension scheme receive life cover of four times their pensionable salary. Employees outside the scheme receive no life cover. Flex recognises that all employees may not want four times cover, and allows those in the pension scheme to trade down to three or two times cover and receive a cash credit instead. Employees not in the pension scheme can buy up to two, three or four times cover at the same rates.

Health care Health care is provided free to employees on the basis of their family status, ie single employees receive single cover, married employees receive married cover and so on. These employees are now able to trade down on the cover for their partner and dependants, and receive a cash credit instead. This may be of particular benefit to an employee whose partner already receives private medical insurance at their place of work. Flex also includes an opportunity for employees to trade up to a higher level health care scheme with a higher financial limit for outpatient care. In addition, Mercury have arranged for employees to have a private medical health screen at a discounted rate. This cost is met by the employee.

Employee cars In addition to the existing company car

scheme, which enables management employees to have a car of their choice, or a cash option, or a combination of the two, Mercury have introduced a lease purchase car scheme which offers all employees a choice of virtually any new car at their own cost. This is operated by the companies who supply the business fleet and offers an alternative to the high street lease purchase schemes.

Dental insurance Mercury currently offers a single level dental scheme which provides reimbursement at NHS levels. Flex introduces an alternative plan providing reimbursement at private treatment cost levels. These costs are met by the employee, but are available at rates below those of external plans.

Annual leave Mercury offers 25 working days' leave to permanent full-time employees but the flex programme will enable employees to vary their leave by up to 5 working days each year. Employees can therefore trade down to 20 days or up to 30. This choice requires the approval of the employee's line manager.

Child care vouchers Vouchers are being launched with flex. They can be used to pay a nursery, childminder, nanny etc, and are free of National Insurance. The employee must agree to relinquish a chosen portion of salary and will receive the vouchers instead. This will give most employees about a 6 per cent saving on child care costs.

Flex packs The flexible benefits programme is being communicated through presentations, posters, the company newspaper and 'flex packs' which contain each employee's personalised choices. These are sent to home addresses, because so many of the flex choices are family decisions. The enrolment process ran for ten weeks. Flex then went live for all Mercury employees to receive independent external financial counselling to help them with their pension choices. This is available on a helpline and through 'surgeries' at Mercury locations.

Communication

Communicating about issues *within* companies rather than from business-to-business or from company to consumer is a growing discipline but not growing fast enough. The normal rules of thumb for consumer marketing tend not to be translated across to internal staff even with consumer-driven companies and consequently many worthy initiatives die on the vine due to a lack of serious internal communication. The investment in time and materials is rarely made, resulting in poorly perceived communication. You need to be clear what messages you wish to give and what response you would hope for.

Saatchi & Saatchi, North America

When Saatchi & Saatchi, the world's biggest advertising agency, decided to introduce a flex plan in 1987 within its North American subsidiary, not everything went according to plan. They only gave themselves three months to complete the implementation and on their own admission did little to consult with employees or think through the communication process. The plan had a disappointing take-up. When they researched the issues, one of the key problems was the workforce's unwillingness to read booklets or long memos on a subject perceived to be boring and irrelevant.

Getting the message across

Like any other marketing plan, you need to examine the target market carefully to determine the type of marketing techniques to use and the approach to take.

The project team approach in the design phase will provide important clues as to what parts of the message to emphasise. The first step could be a features *v* advantages analysis, where key features of the new package are represented as specific advantages, in promotional terms (see Table 6.3).

The next step is to translate those advantages into a variety of media relevant to the employee grade.

Senior staff may well be involved at the concept stage and so be familiar with the plan through board papers, policy meetings or budget proposals. They may not need anything more formal than administrative notes on how to make the choices.

However, they do need to know what elements of the flex plan to highlight and how to present the idea 'down the line' or across the company. Verbal briefings are important but you need more permanent techniques if the 'cascade' of information is going to work. Interactive media are important. Introducing a flex plan is a two-way process between employer and employees. There should be opportunities for dialogue. On the one hand the scheme needs to be 'sold', but equally there are important educational points to be made which do not always strike home first time around. Like advertising, key messages need to be repeated several times before

Staff Incentives and Performance Management Techniques

Table 6.3 Features v Advantages Analysis

Features	Advantages
• Scheme includes all levels	• Staff feel there are no privileged grades
• Pilot test first	• Learn from initial systems or perception problems
• Obligatory membership	• Automatic inclusion from day 1
• 5 new benefits	• Perceived as better value, a bigger package
• Choices can be made on-screen	• Administration is personal/instant/confidential
• Flex plan representative at each site regardless of plan size	• Someone close by who can explain details in person

the messages can be fully understood. Anticipating the extra workload in human resources also needs to be done realistically. If you offer a 'helpline', you should expect least half of the workforce to use it in the initial stages, so gear up for the response adequately.

Promotional Media

The choice of options is huge. The following list offers some suggestions for techniques which can be used:

- one-to-one briefings;
- team briefings;
- large conference;
- video;
- distance learning;
- focus group;
- CD-Rom packages;
- explanatory booklet;
- wall poster;
- workshops;
- audio-cassette;
- telephone helpline;
- payslip inserts;
- business TV.

Depending on the audience, one, some or most of these techniques could be used to get the message across, but set-up costs will argue against many, if the projected audience is small or split across various sites. When Saatchi & Saatchi followed up its initial failure with 22 focus group consultations, the company developed telephone booth style information points where participants were able to ask for additional data about their own situation and make their benefit choices in a confidential environment on demand. Promotion was concentrated on posters, short memos and brief, eye-catching leaflets to get the key points across.

Employees on one site with clear reporting lines may find the cascade approach of team briefings and focus groups (once launched) backed up by noticeboards and explanatory brochures to be an effective combination. PC packages are being used increasingly as a means of providing opportunities for employees to ask 'what if' questions at their own pace, as they consider their selection options, and for them to make their selections confidentially.

In a company with perhaps a dozen or more regional sites, with representatives largely using the regional office as an accommodation address, video may be appropriate to establish senior level commitment and perhaps audio-cassettes for the representatives to use while driving around their territory. Explanatory back-up literature written in a non-technical style should always be made available.

For younger age groups, perhaps working part-time, more interactive promotion may be appropriate. A distance learning programme, either on paper or on screen would encourage more response on an issue perceived to be 'difficult', especially if they tend not to be the main breadwinner. In these cases, the partner should be involved as many benefits could be duplicated and choices need to be based on pooling the knowledge of both partners' benefit systems.

Don't forget those who join after the scheme has been introduced. They will not have the advantage of the initial flush of launch enthusiasm. You need to create a package about flexible benefits as part of your recruitment or induction process so that new recruits become as knowledgeable and confident about the company's flex plan as those who were there from its inception.

Once launched, the key point is to keep communicating during the first year with a peak at the anniversary so as to educate employees, giving them as much information as possible before they make their annual choices. For most people, a flex plan is a very new concept and people need time to understand the consequences of their choices, both in direct financial terms and in lifestyle. For some individuals, the initial attraction of trading some benefits for additional holiday entitlement, for example, may be highly attractive at the time, until the day they could face financial hardship due to a prolonged illness and wish they had been a little more cautious.

THE STAGES OF EFFECTIVE COMMUNICATION

With all communication issues you need to consider the level of understanding of the audience (without being patronising), the content of the message, the medium through which the message is communicated and the timing. Each audience may require a slightly different message on presentation. Each stage of the process may require a different approach. There will be a great deal to communicate at the beginning of the programme, but take care not to congratulate yourself on the amount of material you have produced. People may never get round to reading it, particularly younger, more mobile employees. The main points need to be emphasised verbally, with back-up literature for those who like to take in the information in their own time at their own pace. During the first year, a regular feature in the company newsletter or even an audio-cassette (radio programme style) on a regular basis can be used to feedback some of the main misunderstandings or common queries. It can also be useful to feature testimonials from various types of employee so people can compare choices and discuss the relative merits. At the first and subsequent anniversaries, employees will be preparing to review their options. Face-to-face discussion should be encouraged to reassure those thinking about making some changes. Many companies find a 'clinic' approach helps people make better decisions. The relative merits can be aired, either individually or in a group, with the help of a facilitator, from within the company or from a consultancy.

In this way employees will be happier with their eventual choices and take a real interest in the value of each benefit to their particular current situation. The theory of cognitive dissonance – buyers needing reassurance that they have made the right choice – applies with flex plan choices. Remember to reassure choosers.

SOME COMMON COMMUNICATION ERRORS

- Failure to do enough research.
- Raising expectations in the research phase which cannot be delivered.
- Too much information too quickly.
- Over-reliance on written media (brochures, handouts, booklets).
- Inadequate briefing of local administrators.
- Talking down.
- Not enough relevant examples.
- Too much jargon in the brochure or in presentations.
- No opportunity to get queries answered.
- Slow feedback on choices made (individual statements).
- No communication plan for employees who join mid year.
- Inconsistency of detail across the various media used.
- Poor quality materials (remember, the medium is the message).

Communication is a key element in the flex plan process. Without considerable care in this area, the whole initiative risks being stillborn.

TAX, INSURANCE AND FINANCIAL PLANNING ISSUES

Although these issues will depend on the fiscal situation in each country, the principles remain constant. Because many financial benefits are age related, in particular pensions, health and life assurance, employees doing the same job may not receive the same level of benefit. A 58-year-old man with heart problems will not be able to 'buy' the same amount of life cover for the same price as a 25-year-old amateur athlete. Older employees will have to spend more of their credits on such items, leaving fewer credits available to spend on more discretional items, unless core benefits price this out.

In some schemes, pension contributions are included as a key part of a newly introduced flex plan to make the switch from an expensive pension benefit based on final salary to one based on money purchase. This would be less onerous for the company in years to come. By offering a basic pension benefit for everyone with the flexibility to use other flex plan credits to top it up or use on other flexible benefits, those needing a high rate of pension funding could continue at the old level, with other employees choosing to fund their pension at a lower level.

In other schemes, pension contributions are totally excluded from the flex plan. It may be that the company has a high number of young employees who may not want to spend credits on pensions or, more simply, the company may wish to avoid the administration.

Although medical insurance take-up depends on the level of basic cover available from the state, many employees in the UK are taking on the responsibility of providing additional private health care to avoid the inevitable waiting times within government schemes and to be able to specify a specialist physician.

But diagnostic costs are rising sharply, together with the corresponding monthly premiums. By providing private health care through a flex plan, employees can see the cost in 'credits' spent. Additional costs levied by the provider can be passed on to employees without reflecting badly on the company. The inevitable cross-subsidies between family members and single members will disappear. Employees pay only for their own level of benefit. The company is therefore no longer committed to having to budget for everyone to be covered at the expensive 'family grade' level. In terms of advantages to the company, this is one feature where companies break the link between open-ended commitment to benefit provision and the brave new world of 'defined cost'.

The benefits available under a flex plan are no different from those available under normal benefit schemes. The difference with a flex plan is the visibility of their cost to the employee. Once you have established a cost for each tranche of benefit, any increases in cost to the company or enhancements due to the employee's personal circumstances can be passed directly on to the employee in future years.

Pricing the flex plan

Pricing the flex plan is a complex task and not something to be taken on without some sound professional advice. There are several routes you could take, depending on your overriding reason to offer flexible benefits; pricing is a sophisticated consultancy service which uses proven mathematical models to arrive at appropriate credit levels, but it depends what your objectives are.

- Provide employees with the same level of benefits as before, but with a wider element of choice.
- Reduce the level of benefits offered, but offset the change with a wider range.
- Subsidise older employee costs.
- Communicate the real cost of benefits to employees.
- Buy out old practices and expensive benefits.

Depending on your financial or strategic objectives, the cost of the flex plan will change according to which benefits you include at a standard threshold and which benefits you decide should be purchased on a credit-by-credit basis.

To offset the effects of unwise choices made by employees, you should always identify those benefits which may be subject to adverse selection prior to launch, and assess the likely impact on the overall costs and on the individuals concerned. If initial soundings suggest that the take-up may be adverse, you may need to impose some restrictions on choice or establish a minimum requirement for the advantage of all. But individual pricing helps, as does providing core benefits. You may decide to subsidise regular health checks to promote a healthier workforce which will in time feedback into lower insurance premiums in the future.

Inevitably, there will be winners and losers in any newly formed flex plan. It is essential prior to any announcement that an estimate is made of the benefit/financial change within various sub groups to avoid wholesale rejection of the plan. Extreme cases (those whose benefits are reduced by 1 per cent or more) should be compensated in some other way. If possible avoid introducing the changes at the same time as the annual salary review as 'losers' will compare their loss against their former salary and so feel more disadvantaged than they actually are.

The technique for costing the plan is one of modelling, testing, refitting and remodelling until such time as you are happy with the tolerance levels at the extremes. No scheme will work out perfectly, but with a series of checks and balances, using informed assumptions, you should be able to devise a flex plan to meet most people's perceptions.

ADMINISTRATION

Despite the obvious cost control benefits to the employer and the freedom of choice flex plans offer to employees, many companies are put off at the implementation stage when they come to consider the administration aspects. But going beyond giving everyone the same benefits is bound to be more complex. You need to consider just how much more complex it will be to administer the new benefits.

The first task is to break down the administrative task into bite-sized chunks and apply some common sense. Flex plan administration systems are characterised by four key criteria:

- database format;
- employee selection procedures;
- links with other parts of the business;
- training of administrators.

Database format

Depending on the size and complexity of the scheme, you can choose to set up a manual system, a spreadsheet system, a system integrated with the existing personnel/payroll system or an independent flex plan system. No system is intrinsically better than any other. Your choice depends on what the system will be required to deliver and the funds which are available to pay for it.

You need to consider the IT requirements:

- number of participants;
- range of benefit options;
- frequency of amending choices;
- location of staff;
- existing in-house IT resources, links to other internal systems;
- complexity of the pricing system;

Flexible Benefits

- IT awareness among staff;
- level of database analysis required;
- costs, both for the initial outlay and the maintenance costs.

There are several proprietary software packages available on the market, normally through your flex plan consultant, which will encompass many of the above parameters. An example of such a system is the Flexible Remuneration System from Sedgwick Noble Lowndes; a PC-based package which can also be used for non-flex plans as a benefits management system. It can operate independently or interface with existing human resources systems and can export data or merge with in-house systems such as word processing or desk-top publishing packages.

The key functions include:

- employee data maintenance;
- calculation of credits per employee;
- selection of benefits by employee;
- reports (additions, deletions, cost centre, P11D).

Whichever system you choose, the package should be able to administrate the selection of benefits (and the amount of individual benefit) by employees and report on those selections. The selection process should include an enquiry system so that employees can try out various permutations before deciding on specific choices. Once a selection is made there should be a personal illustration of the impact of choices made and the new benefit levels chosen with any appropriate caveats about an unbalanced selection. The system should also indicate when the benefits will commence. Some may be immediate, at the end of the month or at some future date. In all cases the selection should trigger any relevant changes to payroll and the statutory requirements for employment law reporting.

Employee selection procedures

It is important with any new internal system that you take time to make the system as user-friendly as possible, especially with a subject so little understood as benefits.

The project team needs to decide what would be the best way for employees to make their selections. If the procedure is too complicated, employees will fail to take advantage of flex and you will have incurred considerable consultancy cost for nothing. If the workforce is mature, working in a traditional industrial environment, you may find that manual input on paper is the most attractive way to get participation, although it may be the least efficient. If the workforce is IT-friendly and used to functioning through a networked PC system, then on-screen benefit selection is an obvious route.

You should take care not to lose the human touch. There should always be an opportunity for employees to talk to the designated flex administrator about the choices available before confirming the selection. Not only does it provide reassurance, it can be a useful way for those familiar with the system to pick up any employee difficulties or misconceptions about the flex plan that may have come about through rumour, misinformation or simply poor communication.

Linking flex plans into the business

Because 30 per cent or more of the company's total overhead could be benefits-related, you need to ensure that, whichever system you adopt, the system is compatible with all the associated systems to do with employee costs. There will be reporting implications across a wide spectrum: National Insurance; tax; payroll; statutory reporting; general overheads budget. Because a flex plan involves individuals making personal choices, the final management of the allocation of benefits will be much more complex than before. The full implication of the new reporting requirements need to be examined carefully so that all the loose ends are picked up and pigeon-holed.

Training

Training of the main administrators is crucial, but not just in file maintenance. The site or divisional administrator of the new flex plan will be the representative of all that is good about individual choice of benefits. The flex plan administrator should therefore be articulate about the theory as well as the practice and be an enthusiastic ambassador for the scheme, either on a one-to-one basis or as part of a project team. The administrator should also be experienced enough to anticipate any systems problems when it comes to interfacing with other company-wide packages and report them appropriately so that errors or malfunctions are not ignored.

Running through all four criteria is the link with your benefit providers. All providers need to be consulted in the development of your delivery systems so that the employees are well served.

IS CHOICE OF BENEFITS MOTIVATIONAL?

There is no doubt that for many companies flexible benefits provides a way to be more responsive to the individual's need to take more direct control over benefits due to changing lifestyles. But what part does a flex plan play in the quest for performance improvement?

'Flexing' is in its early days, particularly in the UK. The advantages to both employee and employer have been outlined in this chapter. Because there are so few examples of schemes in the UK up and running, unequivocal proof that retention can be increased, recruitment costs can be lessened and cost control can be improved are at present anecdotal by the standards of science. But if it is clear that used as part of a general company strategy to unlock the potential of individuals to improve their effectiveness at work by making their remuneration more appropriate, then the moral argument has been won.

Whether flexible benefits, as the plans mature, can be used as tactical incentive devices to focus attention on key business issues such as higher key task performance has yet to be tested. There are many situations where offering additional flex plan credits to reward desirable behaviour seems like a perfect method to tie performance to reward in a personally relevant way.

In short, flex plans form part of the motivational jigsaw which, if integrated into a performance improvement culture, could be one of the major driving forces towards higher efficiency. By themselves, at the very least they allow you to control your costs better. If fully integrated, a flex plan could be the catalyst to a workforce transformed by the freedom of personal choice in how they are paid that they improve performance at work in a tangible way.

That has to be a better way to retain employees or recruit new ones in the future, even if at present it cannot be proved.

Summary

- Benefits provided a way to offer staff basic economic security.
- They became a means to attract and retain staff.
- By offering the choice of how much to take of which benefit, a company can be shown to be more responsive.
- Administration and communication are crucial to the sound introduction of flexible benefits.
- It is still early days in the UK to assess the effect of flex plans, but anecdotal evidence suggests they can increase retention and recruiting competitiveness.

7

INCENTIVE TRAVEL: EVERYONE'S TOP REWARD

Holidays are an expensive trial of strength. The only satisfaction comes from survival.
                                                       Jonathan Miller

EXTRAORDINARY REWARDS

After considering cash and benefits as incentives and finding both wanting as motivational tools in isolation, we are left with a myriad of non-cash options to choose from.

But of all the possible non-cash rewards you could offer as part of a motivation programme, a travel experience is by far the most popular. It is also the most expensive. Depending on where you go and what you do, you could be spending anywhere between £500 and £5000 per person. If you consider that professional incentive travel always includes a partner (husband, wife, boyfriend, girlfriend), qualifiers need to have achieved extraordinary levels of performance, simply to make the whole thing pay for itself. It also requires an extraordinary level of logistical planning.

But extraordinary is what incentive travel is all about. Incentive travel is not just an expensive package holiday. There are many tour operators who can supply that product. There are significant features which differentiate incentive travel from promotional or holiday travel. The main difference is that you would normally travel as a

Staff Incentives and Performance Management Techniques

group rather than as an individual, although in the US travel rewards for individuals and their families are often included in incentive travel statistics. But travelling as a group is not the only difference.

A definition may help. This one was compiled by the ITMA (Incentive Travel & Meetings Association) under Max Cuff's chairmanship.

> Incentive travel is that discipline of sales and marketing management which uses promise, fulfilment and memory of an exceptional travel related experience to motivate participating individuals to attain exceptional levels of achievement in their places of work or education.

It comes as a surprise to many potential clients that incentive travel is in fact a marketing technique. Like any other marketing technique it needs to be appropriate, budgeted for and managed effectively.

Incentive travel is by far the most popular reward within the framework of an integrated motivation programme, after cash. But the reasons for this are not simply because travel is expensive and therefore highly valued as a reward.

Travel sits right at the heart of effective motivation for all kinds of psychological reasons. It appeals to all the senses. It offers relaxation from a stressful life. It has 'trophy value'; you can impress the neighbours by talking about where you are going and where you've been. Peer group pressure to qualify with your high achieving colleagues is very strong within a commercial environment. High achievers like to be formally recognised for a job well done and to meet influential senior management. There is team member pressure to 'join the club' and belong to one of the élite. It is also a powerful sales management tool in retaining top achievers until some time after the end of their effort to qualify. It is no accident that most 12-month programmes do not fulfil until 3 or 4 months after the end of the qualification period. This is not only to ensure enough time to make the necessary arrangements. By the time the incentive event is over, based on the previous year's performance, the top achievers are three or four months into the next cycle of qualification and probably already leading the pack. It is difficult to ignore the anticipation of another complimentary long-haul holiday for the sake of a new employer with new products to learn about and no guarantee of repeating success. So people who attend incentive travel events tend to be retained longer than those who do not qualify.

AEG: Off to the Orient

But does it work? AEG, a German-based white goods manufacturer with subsidiaries in the major European countries, ran a four-month campaign aimed at key stockists called 'Off to the Orient'. They had analysed the contribution from their 800 stockists and discovered there were only 200 serious players. The rest were occasional trade purchasers. Of the 200 stockists, the top 40 (20 per cent) produced 80 per cent of the business.

By leaguing stockists into eight turnover bands, they were able to offer a guaranteed trip to Hong Kong for the top five in each league. But the participants in each league differed in number depending on the size of the stockist's historic purchases. The big providers had a one in two chance of qualifying. The smaller providers had a progressively lower chance. In this way AEG were able to satisfy their major purchasers and provide a keen element of competition.

A fast-start award of a weekend in Amsterdam was offered for everyone who achieved target over the first two months of the campaign. Salespeople in the retail outlets could win a series of Chinese-style merchandise awards by picking out a lucky Chinese fortune stick when the field representative called, provided the salesperson had sold an AEG machine during that cycle. The results were impressive. Many of the top stockists increased their purchases by 20 per cent, some as much as 50 per cent. AEG also benefited from the fast-start mechanism by unprecedented levels of immediate sales in a traditionally average retail sales period.

PROMISING THE EARTH

What is meant by 'promise' in Max Cuff's definition of incentive travel? In product terms the destination needs to be sold to the participants *before* they start to compete rather than after the race is over. It is an incentive to promote higher performance, not a reward for achieving whatever would have been achieved anyway. It also has to be recognised that if planned correctly and because of the per head costs, less than 20 per cent of the programme participants will qualify for the incentive trip, so the power of the incentive for most of the participants lies in the anticipation rather than the fulfilment.

The choice of incentive destination starts with what possibilities there may be to promote the venue, even though the majority of participants may never have been there and may never qualify. It follows that not every place in the world can be a universally popular incentive destination. Cities like London, Paris or New York are bona fide world players as far as the image of the destination is concerned. They need little explanation and offer a wide range of attractive features to many levels of participant in many cultures. Other places may in reality be equally fascinating but will need to be promoted in much the same way as any local tourist office would present any location. Evian, for example, on the shores of Lake Geneva is not well known beyond France and Switzerland, but can provide everything necessary for a top-class incentive event. Depending on your perspective, some cold and windy destinations in northern Europe are irresistible to people who live in hot climates, simply because they represent an alternative lifestyle.

It is often said that the best way to promote a destination is to take people there so they can experience it for themselves. This explains why the consumer travel industry spends so much time hosting even the most junior retail travel clerks off peak to their latest products at what seems great expense. It is the only way to get the distributors to know the product. However, with incentive travel, the participants cannot attend the event first and qualify later. For that reason, a clear and objective assessment of how the destination is likely to be perceived has to be made. Paris may be old hat to an experienced group, but to first timers it cannot be beaten. In fact statistically the majority of first time incentive groups out of the UK visit Paris.

Perception is everything

So the motivational power of a destination is concerned more with perception than reality. In other words, for the particular group you wish to motivate the question is whether London/Paris/New York is going to give you the right cluster of perceptions you need to achieve maximum motivation, given the available budget. A recent poll of European meeting planners rated the appeal of conference destinations around the world. Top was Paris, bottom was Glasgow. But in between there were some obvious perceptions and some less obvious misperceptions.

Table 7.1 Appeal of Conference Destination

Destination	Average Score	Destination	Average Score
Paris	8.0	Los Angeles	6.4
Hawaii	7.8	Lisbon	6.4
Hong Kong	7.5	Budapest	6.3
Singapore	7.5	Brussels	6.3
New York	7.5	Edinburgh	6.2
Geneva	7.4	Copenhagen	6.1
London	7.4	Milan	5.9
Cannes	7.3	Stockholm	5.9
Monaco	7.3	Istanbul	5.8
Rome	7.1	Cyprus	5.8
Florence	7.1	Munich	5.8
Nice	7.1	Frankfurt	5.7
Vienna	7.0	Athens	5.6
Amsterdam	6.9	Dublin	5.6
Bangkok	6.8	Luxembourg	5.3
Barcelona	6.7	Marbella	5.3
Berlin	6.7	Helsinki	5.2
Madrid	6.4	Cairo	4.9
Miami	6.4	Dubai	4.3
Zurich	6.4	Glasgow	4.2

Source: Reed International

The top 20 could serve equally well as a list of popular incentive travel destinations, apart from perhaps Geneva which has a more business-like image commensurate with what conference organisers are looking for. Some destinations do not deserve to be perceived so poorly. Dubai at next to bottom is just starting to make itself known to the European market, but offers exceptional incentive travel features to experienced buyers. As with any market, fashions change. In the late 1980s Athens was a popular European destination combining culture and beach-life in a unique way. Through the 1990s, it lost its appeal due to poor publicity about airport safety and the genuinely high levels of pollution in downtown Athens, although a recent ban on private cars has improved this situation. This perception has yet to be reversed. Cape Town is conspicuously absent due to the former political situation in South Africa. Future surveys would certainly show South Africa in the top third of attractive destinations.

The important point for the incentive travel organiser is to keep in touch with the perceptions of the average participant. If the destination is too obscure or snobbish you will lose impact, particularly if you have to labour to explain its attractions. Aspen, Colorado, has been hitting the headlines in recent years, not least due to the patronage of the British royal family and senior members of the US administration. As such it has acquired a higher profile as an incentive destination than it would otherwise. Scottsdale, Arizona has been very well sold to the incentives industry in the UK and hence comes up quite often as a viable US alternative to Las Vegas or San Francisco. But it needs to be sold hard even to experienced buyers whose participants will probably have no immediate perception of what Scottsdale can offer.

Iveco go to Nepal

Logic does not always rule the day. In 1993 Iveco-France (truck manufacturers) ran a highly successful travel incentive built around the creative concept of climbing mountains. Called *'Vaincre'* (to conquer), truck dealers competed over three, three-month stages through a sales product quiz and the appropriate usage of supplied promotional material. The top 30 qualified for a selection of aspirational merchandise or a luxurious weekend away. The top ten won a sporting weekend in Chamonix. The top five would form an accompanied incentive travel trip to Nepal including a visit to the foothills of Mount Everest. Full creative licence was given to the promotion of the campaign including flags to stick on a wallchart, a video about Everest, individual performance bulletins, postcards from the destination and 'expedition notebooks' to record marketing activities completed to date. It worked. Iveco raised their market share by four percentage points to 22.5 per cent over the nine-month programme period.

Easy access

Destination appeal is also about accessibility. If you cannot get there in one flight, the potential qualifiers will not find the destination so attractive. Around the world there are some stunning hotel properties, but lack of international air access is a constant logistical stumbling block to being able to use the property on a consistent basis. Cyprus, for example, has several world class hotels but access is restricted by a relatively small number of scheduled air services from European countries. Although the hotels can deliver the number of luxury rooms required and superb leisure facilities, getting there is less easy than getting to Vienna, for example, particularly from northern Europe which represents the island's main market. Madeira is another destination with great appeal to certain sections of the European market but requires at least one change of plane coming from London Heathrow.

As companies become more security conscious and ask for split flights, so that the risk of losing all their top people on one flight is reduced should there be a plane crash, satisfying the requirement to get everyone to the destination on the same day in time for the inaugural dinner could be a tall order. Getting them all there within 12 hours is fine. To do it within three hours is often impossible.

Promoting the image

To present the promise, you need to promote what is on offer. Incentive travel only exists in the participants' minds until they qualify for the trip. The image of the destination needs to be carefully promoted in the same way that any product would be. Promotion can range from a video or wallposter through to a brochure, local artefact, a postcard from the destination or even an advertisement in the newspaper local to the destination, hoping to welcome company qualifiers next spring! Whatever is decided, there should be a plan to keep the destination high on the agenda of those who could qualify. This is particularly important in the middle stages of the qualification period when interest and enthusiasm are likely to be sagging. Because the budgets for incentive travel are high compared with other sales promotion projects, you need to make the most of your investment. For that reason qualification periods can be anything up to two years. The usual period is 12 calendar months, closely tied into the financial year so that qualification at the year end is related to the general business performance of individuals against their peers.

A promotional plan needs to be drawn up, budgeted for and adhered to, if you are going to achieve your incremental sales objectives. Many programmes suffer from a launch-it-and-leave-it attitude, where all the promotion happens at the beginning of the programme with no coherent messages during the campaign. If you choose a destination with positive perceptions you should have a lot to say during the qualification period to encourage participants to focus their efforts on achieving higher performance.

A typical incentive travel promotion plan would be high on gloss, competition detail, qualifiers' names and photos, with specific timings about the itinerary left until nearer the end of the qualifying period.

TYPICAL INCENTIVE TRAVEL PROMOTION SCHEDULE

Oct–Dec	Development, costing, design of materials
January	Launch at a sales conference. Brochure, video, monthly competition bulletin
March	Teaser from the destination. Newsletter promoting hotel
June	Teaser, mid year results, Newsletter promoting destination. Video to support destination message
October	Teaser, 'Fast Finish double points promotion'. Newsletter promoting pro rata qualifiers. Draft itinerary
January	Final results, congratulations bulletin, joining instructions for qualifiers. (Launch of next year's programme)

It is tempting to think that if you promote the destination well enough, the event will take care of itself. The incentive travel experience must go beyond expectations to the point that the event becomes the best advertisement to requalify for the following year. There is nothing more dispiriting than a product which does not at the very least meet expectations, especially if you have made an extraordinary personal effort to qualify.

MAKING INCENTIVE TRAVEL DIFFERENT

As a product, incentive travel is very different from a package holiday, even though the hotel and destination may well be the same. This is not only because you travel as part of a group. It is all about enhancing the travel experience.

The group nature of incentive travel means that enhancements can be made to the travel experience that are not normally available to the individual holidaymaker, without considerable organisation and expense.

Off-airport check-in

You can arrange for qualifiers' luggage to be checked in at a nearby hotel so that they do not have to queue up with everyone else at the terminal. Airlines at busy airports often prefer to operate in this way as it means less administration at the terminal check-in desk and less crowding in the departure hall.

The advantages for the organiser are what makes incentive travel different. Qualifiers feel they have been singled out for special treatment. They are transferred to the terminal together as a group, so there is no possibility of them getting lost. They can begin to socialise with other members of the group. This getting-to-know-each-other process is an important element of what incentive travel offers. If the group can establish an early common bond, they tend to enjoy the experience much more. As many groups will be from the same company or industry, they will already know more about each other's lifestyle than most holiday-making individuals, meeting for the first time.

They can relax about the ticketing and travel arrangements as they know this is being handled by the professional group organiser. From the participant's angle, the administrative detail involved in international travel is largely taken care of.

We used to handle an annual convention for a very large IT company. Each year we would take 300–400 senior managers and salespeople to a European destination for 4 or 5 nights, staying at a top-class hotel. Part of the post-event research process was to interview at random some of the participants to establish any improvements we could make for the following year. I flew to Belfast with the researchers to sit in on a few of the sessions. When asked a general question about the appeal of incentive travel to top achievers the local manager said: 'You know, I spend most of my working day taking difficult decisions, dealing with people problems, worrying about the market and planning for an uncertain and unpredictable future. As soon as I check in for the convention, I know I can take my brain out of gear and not have to think or plan or worry – just enjoy myself. It's only for a week or so each year, but I really do look forward to being organised by someone else for a change.'

From the organiser's viewpoint an off-airport check-in means they know who has checked in before the departure to the airport, and so can take contingency action for named and identified latecomers or no-shows. If the qualifiers have been invited to stay overnight the day before departure (an early morning check-in may be necessary), they have an opportunity to get to know their fellow qualifiers and the company hosts. The organiser can make any announcements, introduce themselves and their role, and double-check any last-minute queries, particularly to do with passports or the return itinerary.

If the destination requires entry visas, the incentive travel organiser will normally organise the administrative detail and pay any fees due, for later reimbursement from the sponsoring company.

Enhancing the journey

Incentive travel includes negotiating the best possible deal on the aircraft, but not just the price. Special needs such as aisle seats, window seats, more leg room, special diets or non-smoking can be requested long before the group checks in. This means that qualifiers can enjoy a more comfortable journey than simply taking pot-luck at the check-in desk or, worse still, being bumped off the flight due to over-booking by the carrier.

If the flight is chartered for the exclusive use of the group at a specific departure time, personalised headrests, meals, particular drinks and even particular video entertainment can be arranged. One group of automotive dealers who were due to be going home on a long-haul flight were bemoaning the fact that due to the gala dinner the night before travelling, they would miss a world championship boxing match. We recorded the fight on video in the hotel during the gala dinner and after the evening meal on board the overnight charter the next day, we ran the video of the previous night's boxing. The qualifiers were overwhelming in their gratitude. The idea to do it was priceless. But it cost the client no more than the price of a blank videotape.

More travellers does not always mean less cost

One common misconception among incentive travel buyers is that the more people you book on a flight, the lower the price. With most other commodities, there would be a discount for bulk purchase. There is always a group rate which is lower than the published fare, but higher numbers does not automatically lead to a further reduction in price. An airline seat has a finite life. There are only so many seats on one aircraft flying from one destination to another. When the airline works out its yield – how much revenue it needs on that particular flight to make a profit – it knows a certain proportion of the market will buy a certain number of seats at a specific price: First Class; Business; Economy; APEX; Stand-by. It is not unusual for one Boeing 747 to be carrying passengers who paid 25 or more different prices to go from London to New York on the same flight.

Although incentive group fares are negotiated through the special groups department and will normally be cheaper than published scheduled fares, how much cheaper depends on the availability of seats at that cheaper price (they know a guaranteed number of business seats will be sold in the last few days before departure from their bookings history database). It may be that on the scheduled flight you have identified as being perfect for your group, the airline will only allow you to take 40 seats at the discounted rate, because they know they can sell the balance at a higher price. So you either pay the higher price, split the flight with another carrier or cost out a charter for the whole group.

Buying airline space is one of the great black arts of incentive travel. Very often it is not what you know, but who the organiser knows within the airline which can secure the best deal for the client.

Charter options

An entire library could be produced on the intricacies of aeroplane charters, but as far as incentive travel is concerned the relevant factors are:

Staff Incentives and Performance Management Techniques

1. Number of travellers (pax).
2. Budget.
3. Availability of aircraft.
4. Accessibility of destination.

You may find you are unable to buy enough seats at the price you want using scheduled services. There may not be a convenient departure time for eventual arrival in the destination. In the case of an island or remote venue, there may not be a scheduled flight on the day you want.

Chartering is an alternative option. However, you pay a fixed price for the plane based on fuel costs so you need to find a plane which most nearly suits the size of your group to get the best value cost per head. Because it is most unlikely you will be bringing qualifiers back home the moment they arrive at the destination, you will usually pay for the 'empty leg'. Occasionally, the charter company may have another client with similar numbers who could take up the empty leg. But this is unlikely, unless it is a series of charters, as would happen during the holiday season for a tour operator, so the cost of fuel for the return flight has to be factored in. In general, chartering is an expensive option. Availability of a suitable aircraft may not be confirmed until a few weeks before departure, such is the nature of the ad hoc charter market. Some corporate clients find this an unacceptable arrangement, as it always carries the risk that no suitable plane can be found within the available budget, leaving qualifiers stranded at the airport.

The destination decision may well depend on flight accessibility so careful thought needs to be given to the practical question of whether the qualifiers can actually get there comfortably and at the right price.

Baggage

One of the banes of international travel when you travel as an individual is baggage. Incentive travel is about treating the qualifiers as VIP guests and smoothing their passage through the unavoidable procedures of travelling. A professional incentive travel organiser, as mentioned above, will arrange for baggage to be 'checked in' at an off-airport hotel so that qualifiers can go straight through customs. At the destination, baggage has to be personally identified in the normal way in the baggage hall, but the incentive group organiser can often arrange for porters to come 'airside' to take the baggage away if permitted and deliver it to the hotel by special baggage vans. By doing this, the baggage can get to the hotel before the qualifiers, enabling them to be delivered to rooms in time for the qualifiers' arrival, if logistics allow.

So, no struggling with your suitcases from customs to the taxi-rank and then wondering on arrival at the hotel how long the porters will take delivering them to your room.

Hotel check-in

Checking in at a hotel is often cited in research as being something guests consider a necessary evil. The proliferation of 'preferred guest' schemes for frequent business travellers offering instant check-in facilities in the form of a pre-prepared guest envelope similar to the system used by car hire firms is one way to combat this. Incentive groups already benefit from this system. The group organiser will have sent a rooming list to the hotel some days before departure. While the group is in the air, the hotel will be allocating names to rooms. Sometimes, if the hotel is at low capacity, the rooming allocation can even be done the day before the group travels, providing the opportunity for the organiser to write the actual room numbers on the baggage tags as they are checked in prior to departure. This speeds up the porterage considerably at the destination, especially if the organiser has promised a better than average tip for prompt delivery of the group's bags.

It is a source of constant wonder to me around the world how adept hotel porters can be at recognising items of baggage at a glance by noting mentally some feature of the baggage with the personality of the owner. However, I remember one occasion when we managed to do completely the wrong thing (see the Volvo case history in Chapter 1). We had organised a three-month incentive campaign with the top qualifiers travelling to Venice on the Orient Express. Part of the incentive programme was a 'fast start' award of a set of Orient Express baggage for anyone who achieved 100 per cent of their first month's target. Unfortunately they all did!

The result was that everyone who qualified for the trip had identical Orient Express luggage. If you have ever arrived in Venice by train, you will know that the baggage is piled up in a big heap at the end of the platform on disembarkation and you simply claim your suitcase from the baggage mound. Fortunately for the qualifiers it was our job to transfer the baggage so we were the ones who had to wade through 50 identical sets of luggage and allocate each of them to the relevant qualifier's room. Clearly the organiser can never be *too* prepared and should always be ready for unexpected eventualities.

Saving time

On arrival at the hotel (the baggage having been delivered earlier by separate transport), qualifiers should be able to pick up their keys and hotel information at a check-in desk, separate from the main hotel reception desk, often manned by client company staff. This provides a friendly and trouble-free welcome without any potential language difficulties or delays. Often on arrival a cocktail party will be organised in a private part of the hotel to allow a little more time for baggage to be delivered to rooms, for the hosts to make a brief welcome speech, and for qualifiers to relax and take in their new surroundings.

It used to be the done thing to personalise the hotel, so that when the group arrived there was something familiar to see. Typically the hotel lobby would carry company logo banners or there would be a local band playing welcome songs behind a huge company flag.

On one occasion I put a group into a beach resort where all the rooms had balconies overlooking a spectacularly wide pool, not visible from the lobby area. We took the decision not to put up big banners and logos, as the group felt they did not want to be identified as being part of a convention. They were an upmarket, sophisticated crowd.

But the organiser asked us to do something to acknowledge that the group had arrived. So, when the qualifiers walked out on to their balconies for the first time to admire the view, they would naturally look down on the pool area. In the middle of the pool we had constructed the company logo in flowers and floated them on the pool surface as a welcome gesture.

Dinearounds

For some people a daunting aspect of foreign travel is where to eat outside the hotel. As part of an incentive group, eating out in professionally vetted restaurants with local atmosphere becomes a pleasure rather than a trial. Dinearound events are set up, and three or four high quality restaurants are chosen. Qualifiers can choose which restaurant they prefer from supplied prospectuses on the welcome desk. Often they will arrange to go with a group of other qualifiers, sit at the same table and make an evening of it. Company executives will be instrumental in making everyone feel involved by checking the bookings and hosts can make new qualifiers feel welcome by inviting them to 'their' restaurant to introduce them to other qualifiers. No one would be left on their own, unless they wanted to be.

Special excursions and activities

Every incentive destination will afford opportunities to do some sight-seeing. By their very nature, there will be places any tourist could visit. But incentive travel organisers will work with local ground agents to ensure that if there is a chance to do or see something not normally available to the tourist, they will arrange it.

In terms of a venue for dinner it could be a government building in Eastern Europe, a private chateau in the Loire Valley, an exclusive art gallery in Athens or a film star's home in California. Instead of a coach tour, individual transport with or without chauffeur can be organised, with perhaps a few off-the-beaten track places to visit pointed out.

For example, a jeep or mini-moke safari in Barbados is a relaxed way to explore this relatively small Caribbean island. Qualifiers are each assigned an open-top jeep and a sealed envelope containing the questions about the history or culture of the island. With careful planning, the questions can be framed so as to ensure a three or four-hour round trip, ending up at a specific restaurant for a group lunch. Qualifiers can operate independently or split up into teams to encourage a competitive edge. For more enterprising groups, cryptic clues can be set which may involve questioning local inhabitants on things only a local would know.

In some parts of the world it is possible to farm small groups out to spend an evening with a local family to see how the local people really live. This provides some fascinating insights into a country you may only ever visit once in your life. It also allows some money to go back into the local economy, other than through the cash registers at the hotel bar.

SOME UNUSUAL INCENTIVE TRAVEL ACTIVITIES

- Dinner in a tent near Muscat.
- Whale hunting off Vancouver.
- Private charter of US presidential yacht.
- Helicopter landing on the deck of an aircraft carrier.
- Breakfast on the banks of the Zambezi.
- Vintage car rally.
- Lunch on the Great Wall of China.
- 'Jailhouse Rock' party on Alcatraz.
- Police bike escort in New Orleans from airport to hotel.
- Murder Mystery on the Orient Express.
- A real diamond in your cocktail in Amsterdam.
- Dragon boat racing in Hong Kong.
- Playing soccer with Pele.
- Towel party in a Turkish bath.
- Attacked by Saracens in the Jordanian desert.
- Dinner with the Inuit in an igloo.
- Sailing a 19th-century square-rigger.

The range of bespoke activities for incentive groups is restricted only by the imagination of the organiser and the budget of the sponsoring company.

The conference session

During the 1980s it was fashionable to pretend there would be a conference session during the overseas event, in the mistaken belief that the event could be written off against company tax. It was also hoped that individual qualifiers could avoid personal tax if the event was promoted as a business conference or seminar rather than a competition prize.

Tax regimes vary and are currently in a state of flux around the world regarding incentive travel. However, in the US, most of Europe and in Australia, all incentive travel events based on competitive qualification are taxable as benefits to the participant and, in some cases, the partner. Legislation and enforcement has become much tighter in recent years with some major corporations having to dig deep into reserves to pay tax liabilities stretching back several years, following an investigation by the tax authorities.

The result has been a decrease in the number of incentive travel clients who run a conference session, now that there is no fiscal advantage. It is an opportunity wasted. The conference session, however short, allows the company to recognise publicly its top achievers, encourages active participation in corporate aims from the partners and binds the group together. Cottrell in *Social Facilitation* (1978) studied the specific effect of the mere presence of others on individual performance. He concluded that when two or more act together, the intensity of their individual behaviour often increases. Individual goal setting and motivation can be vastly improved by insisting on a conference session, even though there may be little on the agenda which is serious business information.

Partners should be included so that more understanding of the company partners' contribution to the corporation's aims is possible. It also reinforces the virtuous circle of achievement, recognition, support and achievement.

Gala dinner

The night before departing for home, the incentive organiser will normally be required to arrange the gala dinner. This is an opportunity to pull all the qualifiers and their partners together, make a few speeches, perhaps present awards to top achievers, take some photographs and consolidate all the special treatment the qualifiers have enjoyed during the previous few days. Often, due to the large numbers involved, a private cabaret and band can be organised for relatively low cost per person. Each group will respond differently so careful thought must be given to what would be appropriate. The possibilities range from a local after-dinner speaker to an internationally known pop group. But, whoever is chosen, the staging implication needs to be thought through. Sound and lighting equipment could cost more than the cabaret fee in some countries, particularly if the audience is a large one.

One year we organised a gala dinner around the pool of the Astir Palace Hotel, on the Greek coast near Athens. But there was not enough floor space to accommodate the cabaret artiste and her band who were flown in especially. The only solution was to build a staging platform over part of the pool. With the judicious use of coloured theatrical lighting and the existing pool illumination, it proved to be a spectacular gala dinner showpiece which will stay in the memories of those who participated for many years to come.

Extended stays

One of the hidden advantages of qualifying for an incentive travel trip as a participant is free air transport to and from the destination. This leads inevitably to the opportunity to extend the length of time a qualifier could stay in the destination or indeed travel on from there to another destination before returning home. This is particularly attractive on long-haul incentives where the expense and travelling effort has already taken place. Open-jaw air tickets – where qualifiers can enter a country through one airport and exit through a different airport in the same country at no extra cost – enable add-ons to be a highly economic way to enhance the reward.

It is not unusual for the incentive organiser to offer extended stays for a small administrative fee, often in the form of three or four extension packages. Sometimes, an individual itinerary can be organised outside specific add-on packages, but it can be expensive if it involves forfeiting the group return air fare because you are returning from a different part of the world or country.

Extended stays can be an incentive in themselves. Qualifiers with relatives in Australia may consider an incentive to the Far East as part-funding to visit their family, and as such will have a powerful influence on work rate and performance, especially if the partner is pushing the participant to qualify.

Making incentive travel special

Throughout an incentive travel event there will be opportunities to enhance the experience for qualifiers, depending on the available budget. A visit to a vineyard could be made special by giving a free bottle of wine. A tour of a cathedral could be enhanced by a complimentary copy of the glossy guide in the appropriate language. The traditional turn-down of the bed-covers could be accompanied by a small gift of local origin as a surprise for qualifiers who may have been out all day following their own itinerary. It has become almost obligatory to provide a partner's gift to be placed at their place at the gala dinner, even if none of these other enhancements are made.

The guiding principle is to do as much as possible to ensure that the qualifiers are made to feel special, particularly the partners who may have had to make many personal sacrifices during the year in order that the potential qualifier can reach the required standard. The budget is less important than the investment in the future morale of that qualifier to continue to achieve those standards within the framework of the sponsoring company.

Making the memory last

Most companies who use incentive travel for promoting performance improvement stress the effectiveness of marketing the event to those who did not qualify as well as those who did. If incentive travel is being used as a medium-term technique – not just for one isolated campaign – you should invest in providing memories of the event. As we know from personal experience, holiday memories as well as suntans fade rapidly once you are back at work. It is vital to keep that memory alive to encourage the continuation of those improved levels of performance for the subsequent year.

A photo album is one way to keep the memories fresh. A photographer could be engaged to cover the entire event or specific activities in the programme. An album would then be presented to each qualifier at the end of the event as a souvenir. A less expensive variation is a gala dinner individual, table or group photograph presented in a stylish frame with the destination name and year of qualification.

For those who did not qualify, the photographs can be turned into a glossy magazine or a slide show with testimonials from the qualifiers to help promote the following year's destination.

Increasingly, video records are being kept so that the sounds as well as the sights can be captured. Video is much more powerful than print at a conference or launch event in helping communicate the atmosphere and cameo of the event to those who did not attend. Video copies ensure that the non-qualifying partner or colleague may get to see what went on and, we hope, encourage the partner to qualify during the following year. The objective of the video would be to recognise publicly as many qualifiers as

Staff Incentives and Performance Management Techniques

possible rather than be an amateur travelogue, so careful editing is required to ensure every qualifier and partner is shown.

TRENDS IN INCENTIVE TRAVEL

According to recent market surveys, incentive travel is here to stay and in general is growing faster than the economies in which it is used. But any predictions or trends need to be viewed in the context of the particular outbound market.

In the US, the market is estimated at £4,000 million, growing at between 5 and 15 per cent. In the UK the market is much smaller, at some £500 million, Germany comes next in Europe at around £450 million. Outbound from the UK, there is a marked degree of seasonality with around 30 per cent travelling between March and May, 25 per cent between September and November, and the balance evenly spread.

Usage of incentive travel as a technique is a function of the development of the economy, population and geographical location. Not everyone goes to the same destination in the same numbers from the same places. Certainly within Europe, destination trends depend as much on who your neighbour is and your colonial heritage as the objective appeal of the destination.

Table 6.2 Where do Europeans Go?

Country	First Market	%	Second Market	%
Belgium	Netherlands	43	Germany	15
Denmark	Germany	36	Sweden	21
Germany	Netherlands	18	US	13
Greece	Germany	24	UK	20
Spain	UK	32	Germany	28
France	UK	17	Germany	15
Ireland	UK	61	US	14
Italy	Germany	42	UK	8
Netherlands	Germany	49	UK	11
Portugal	UK	31	Germany	16

Source: Touche Ross

Within Europe there is a trend to go to your nearest neighbour first, then somewhere culturally opposite (Spain to Germany, Portugal to UK). Beyond Europe, accessibility comes into its own. If the airlinks are in position on a scheduled basis, then destination choice is tied to frequency of flights and socially acceptable timetables. With the Caribbean, for example, UK groups would normally choose Barbados on British Airways. The French would opt for St Lucia on Air France. The Dutch would go on KLM to the Dutch Antilles. The air schedules for each domestic carrier are well established in these former colonies. In 1994 the top outgoing incentive destination from Italy was the US, but it had nothing to do with air access. Italy was competing in the soccer World Cup.

INDIVIDUAL INCENTIVE TRAVEL

One significant trend is the growth of individual travel as an incentive. Strictly speaking this is not incentive travel, in terms of what the product characteristics should be. But in the US over one-third of all reward travel is individual with over 60 per cent of US companies claiming to use it as a motivational device. This trend can be linked to the growth of flex plans (see Chapter 6) where performance related points can be spent on family holidays rather than items like pensions or meal vouchers. Neither flex plans nor individual reward travel have yet made significant in-roads into the European market, but it may only be a matter of time.

From research in the US, we know that over 50 per cent of American qualifiers for incentive travel trips are repeat qualifiers. Everyday experience in Europe would seem to bear this out as a characteristic feature. The implication is that to achieve similar levels of performance improvement, creativity and analysis in the choice of destination is of paramount importance. Creativity includes the trend towards involvement of the qualifiers in some unique activity as part of the event, rather than simply organising a passive tour. This is particularly true of European qualifiers who tend to travel abroad much more than their US counterpart. They may be visiting a destination for the second or third time and so will need a more creative activity or special venue than is normally provided to even the wealthy tourist.

Since the late 1980s there has been a reciprocation between the US and Europe in terms of preferred incentive destination. The combination of the 1990 Gulf War and lower air fares across the Atlantic has resulted in an unprecedented enthusiasm for American destinations from European buyers which looks set to last for many years. Americans have always come to Europe in droves, more so than to the nearby Caribbean, although media attention concerning terrorism or conflict is much more likely to put off the American qualifier than the European qualifier, when it comes to destination choice.

SIGNIFICANT PRODUCT FACTORS

Although this chapter sets out what characterises successful incentive travel and some market statistics, it is worth taking note of what the qualifiers say. If they are not motivated to requalify, then the product needs to be examined. Apart from the choice of destination, the significant elements of the incentive travel experience can be listed as follows:

1. Facility to bring the partner/spouse.
2. Recognition of achievement.
3. Free time in itinerary.
4. Hotel facilities.
5. Travel time.

These often cited features of successful incentive travel will be true to varying degrees depending on the qualifier profile. It is important to recognise that the hotel facilities are of more concern to qualifiers than the destination itself. In research conducted at the University of Surrey 'hotel facilities' came top of the list of major factors from UK-based incentive travel buyers, scoring twice as important as cultural backdrop or even the presence of a beach.

As people become more individual in their leisure tastes and more insular (take-away meals, home videos, personal stereos), group travel may well decline as a percentage of expenditure on rewards.

There is certainly dramatic evidence in the US that individual or family-orientated holiday rewards is growing fast, as much as 30 per cent of all holiday rewards, suggesting a mature product. Within Europe group incentive travel is still in its mid growth phase, although market evidence from France and Italy reveals that individual incentive travel is becoming a significant part of the required reward fulfilment proposal.

In global terms in excess of 15 per cent of the world's gross national product is involved with travel. In many countries travel and tourism is the biggest single employer. Growth in incentive travel, for both individuals and groups, is widely reported to be between 5 and 15 per cent, year on year, largely linked to a more travel and leisure-hungry economically developing world.

However, integrated motivation agencies would not recognise themselves as being part of the travel industry. Incentive travel will never account for more than 25 per cent of their total turnover, as we have already acknowledged that incentive travel is a marketing technique. Fulfilling the travel elements is incidental to the main task of motivating campaign participants to higher levels of job competence and performance improvement.

OTHER MEANS OF TRANSPORT

Trains . . .

In considering incentive travel as a product a brief word about trains is useful. Trains, which you can either charter or purchase individual tickets for, have limited use as a means of getting from one location to another. However, they can enhance a ground programme considerably, offering panoramas of a landscape often not possible by road. The journey from Montreux to Gstaad in Switzerland is not particularly remarkable by road but, by train, the climb up into the high valleys offers unparalleled views of Lake Geneva, made even more memorable if you can use the train's newly restored Belle Epoque carriages.

The international success of the now restored Venice–Simplon Orient Express has given rise to many copycat products which sell well within their own incentives market (examples are the Palace on Wheels in India or the Andalusian Express in Spain).

But a note of caution should be sounded. Trains in all countries are run by strict timekeepers and custodians of protocol. You have to fit into their criteria, not the other way round. This can mean long waiting periods in sidings for no apparent reason, sequestering of specific trains for government use, and possibly questionable catering and service. You should check rigorously any get-out clauses in the event that your charter contract does not meet your expectations.

... and boats

Chartering boats is not new in incentive travel. It has become a standard element in any coastal or island-based programme. But using large commercial cruise ships for group incentives is relatively new. This is in line with the significant growth trend of consumer take-up of cruising, particularly with younger people. The advantage to the professional incentive organiser is tight control of the budget. Most cruise packages include virtually unlimited food and a generous drink allowance, complimentary on-board entertainment, with evening cabaret and a captive audience. As most cruise itineraries involve sailing at night and anchoring off-shore or in part during the day, the ship becomes a floating hotel, with a different destination each day.

But, as with all things nautical, some people react badly to being at sea, however gentle the motion (almost imperceptible with the largest vessels). Others may feel 'hemmed-in' by being in such close proximity to other people. But in reality most research comparing expectations and experience of cruising shows that guests often comment how 'few' people they thought there were on board and how much more they enjoyed the experience than they expected.

You may also need to consider flight access and sailing times. If there are outbound flight delays, the ship will not wait for your group. Equally if the ship docks late at its final port of call, you could find you have lost your scheduled air seats home.

Table 7.3 UK Cruise Statistics 1986–93

	1986	1987	1988	1989	1990	1991	1992	1993
Total UK residents taking cruises	91,500	128,500	152,140	168,400	186,490	193,010	228,728	264,940
Ex UK cruises	40,900	51,440	50,300	52,650	47,230	65,678	66,866	80,568

From these figures it is clear that the cruising concept is here to stay.

Staff Incentives and Performance Management Techniques

FORWARD PLANNING OF DESTINATIONS

There is a temptation when planning your first incentive travel event to go for the most prestigious venue available. It is natural to want to achieve the biggest impact. However, incentive travel is often a medium- to long-term technique which, if executed well, you will want to repeat. You need to consider carefully an outline plan for subsequent years.

For example, within Europe Monte Carlo in year one would be difficult to follow up in year two within Europe to an unsophisticated audience. A more gradual progression over four years may be more appropriate as aspirations and expectations rise.

Incentive Travel Progression

Year 1	*Year 2*	*Year 3*	*Year 4*
Paris	Vienna	Rome	Monte Carlo

Inevitably you may consider medium or long-haul destinations once the nearer destinations have been used. Some experienced buyers into their tenth or more incentive travel event deliberately adopt a short-haul/long-haul rotation year on year, known to the participants, which allows them to 'come back' from long-haul to short-haul without fear of demotivation.

Other users run long-haul destinations for the very top echelon, with short-haul destinations for the lower level of qualifiers. Another technique is to arrange extensions at the same venue for the very highest achievers by three or four days. Or they could fly on to another destination when the main group has returned home.

Whichever combination is used, each has its advantages and disadvantages, and these can be discussed with the incentives consultancy at the planning stage.

The key point is not to go too far too soon and choose somewhere the participants will feel comfortable. A 5 star hotel is no good if the main attraction of the event is social gatherings in the bar. The price of a round of drinks will become a hot topic of conversation which the organiser and the sponsor could do without.

A FINAL WORD ABOUT PURCHASING

As with the purchase of any promotional supply, you need to ensure that you get what you expected to get for the price you expected to pay. You necessarily take a risk when you buy overseas services because the price fluctuates according to the relative strength or weakness of that country's currency compared with your own. It is always wise to check the record of currency stability over the previous few years and either create a contingency fund or buy forward at today's prices to protect the overall budget. In some cases you will simply have to accept price changes, such as the unilateral imposition of purchase tax, brought about by changes of government or fiscal policy.

Another element is the stability of the organisations from whom the various components are purchased. No supplier is a sure-fire, safe bet. Hotels and airlines, as well as consultancies and agencies, have all gone into liquidation in the past. You need to ensure your company is protected against loss through prudent bonding or simply checking each supplier's professional indemnities. There will always be bad debts in business, but with incentive travel the losses could be very expensive if one of the suppliers happens to go out of business the day before you travel or, even worse, during the event.

Check your supplier's financial protection policies before you sign, just to be on the safe side.

Staff Incentives and Performance Management Techniques

SUMMARY

- Incentive travel is by far the most popular motivation reward after cash.
- Destination selection is an art as well as a science. Perception is everything.
- Ensure there is a planned promotional programme to enhance the destination appeal.
- The incentive travel product is not simply a more expensive consumer holiday product.
- Consider how you can create memories to encourage requalification the following year.
- Protect your company against the possible financial downside of dealing with foreign suppliers or small UK agencies.

8

MERCHANDISE

With all my worldly goods I thee endow.
The Marriage Service

It is a significant fact that, although travel is highly perceived by participants as the most preferred reward choice after cash, much more money is spent on non-travel items.

Most people start with merchandise when they construct their first incentive programme. The reason is not hard to find. Incentive travel is a big ticket item per head (double if you include a partner), and is mainly used in industries where the volume of sales and product margins are high.

Not every type of company can afford hosted travel events. In a survey of 'motivation agencies' in the UK, conducted by *Conference & Incentive Travel Magazine* (February 1995), only 25 to 30 per cent of total motivation agency turnover was deemed to be incentive travel, leaving a significant amount being spent on other reward media. By a process of elimination this means merchandise, vouchers and events.

MERCHANDISE CATALOGUES

Background

E F Macdonald (US) were reputedly the first full service motivation agency, offering a range of merchandise from catalogues in return for participant product sales. The pioneering campaigns were conducted in the US, initially for automotive salespeople and then more widely for any type of salesperson. In the boom years after the Second World War, rising living standards and the growth of conspicuous consumption meant that offering specific items for sales achievements made perfect sense. Being the first to acquire the latest home appliance was the upwardly mobile thing to do.

The very latest electronic gadgets, labour-saving devices or designer goods could be packaged together as a merchandise catalogue, sold for a nominal sum to the client to distribute to participants, with a simple leaflet explaining how many 'points' were required for each item. The more you sold, the more reward you earned.

In the heyday of catalogue programmes, motivation houses and incentive agencies would buy stock at wholesale prices, storing the goods at distribution centres to dispatch to campaign claimants. By selling the goods on to clients at retail prices less a small discount they could make significant profit margins. However, in the late 1980s such holding of stock became gradually less viable. Participants had become much more discerning, considering the price and value of catalogue goods, comparing items with what was readily available from their local stores. The wider distribution of consumer goods, particularly from out-of-town sites and superstores has meant that speed of delivery has become a key factor, as incentive organisers try to close the gap between the desired behaviour pattern and the reward. In theory, the quicker, the better.

As an alternative to holding stock, with all the inherent risks of being stuck with unpopular or obsolete items, some motivation houses set up rolling accounts with the big mail order catalogue companies (like Grattan, Great Universal Stores, Freemans) to supply goods on a JIT (just in time) basis, through specific 'incentive teams' within the mail order companies. However, the drop in demand during the early 1990s caused mail order companies to reduce the range of items available and in some cases cease the service altogether.

The rise of UK store vouchers with their quasi-cash advantages – any denomination, easy distribution, wide range of redemption possibilities – triggered a reappraisal of 'the merchandise catalogue' as a product to deliver reward. It is well known that, given an equal choice between merchandise from a catalogue and vouchers, over 75 per cent of participants invariably choose retail vouchers.

Advantages and disadvantages

But before we condemn all merchandise schemes out of hand it is worth outlining the advantages and disadvantages of merchandise catalogues and merchandise schemes in general.

Advantages	Disadvantages
• Show each item on offer	• Often a limited range
• Colour presentation	• Cost of colour catalogue
• Distribution of catalogue by mail	• Impersonal
	• Difficult to assess real value
• Items priced in 'points'	• Delays in delivery
• No need to visit shop	• Lack of client 'ownership'
• Minimal client administration	• Inconvenient to return goods
• Transit repair guarantees	
• Lower costs	• Many goods unbranded

From an incentive organiser's viewpoint catalogues are simple to purchase and distribute, but there are some significant disadvantages for participants. The most obvious factor is the delay in distribution of the goods. It normally takes two to three weeks after the qualifying period to confirm sales made. In most programmes, a communication is then dispatched to the participant, saying how many points have been won. The participant then chooses an award by completing a claim form which is then mailed to the distribution/fulfilment house. Unless stock is being held by the fulfilment house (less and less common) an order will then be dispatched to the item stockist. As such items tend to be 'picked' on a cycle basis, the order may have to wait for the next picking cycle. In some cases, the item requested may not be in stock. The item then needs to be delivered by road under contract to the claimant. No wonder most catalogue schemes carry the proviso of 28 days for delivery.

In commercial terms it has to be said that for the merchandise supplier incentive-related merchandise is a very small market compared with the entire consumer mail order market in the UK. This is reflected in the less than perfect delivery concessions made by the supplying companies. It all boils down to what represents core business for the supplier. Unless the product supplier specialises in 'incentive reward products', there will always be this tension between supplying mass market products to retail outlets and supplying incentive rewards to individual home addresses on an irregular basis.

Another problem often perceived by participants is the limited range of goods being offered. This stems from the fact that the incentive organiser is often working six to nine months in advance of the redemption process. Many campaign participants tend to accumulate their reward points during the campaign and spend them at the end of the campaign. To ensure that participants can actually receive the items they have worked so hard for, the supplier needs to guarantee that the items in the catalogue will actually be available in sufficient quantities. As most mail order companies contract for stock twice a year for consumers, incentive participants would not be able, in most cases, to obtain automatically the items in the launch catalogue. The solution? A limited range of goods is offered by the mail order companies or other suppliers, comprising items they can guarantee to have in stock. The result? A rather bland selection of middle-of-the-road items which neither inspire nor excite higher level participants.

Catalogue production costs

Colour brochures are expensive to produce and the more transparencies there are per page, the more expensive the brochure. Catalogues contain the worst possible scenario if you want to keep incentive promotional costs down. Lots of separate transparencies means lots of detailed copy and short print runs. (Most client campaigns require less than 1000 copies of the promotional material.)

One way to circumvent this problem has been to use the supplier's catalogue which has been produced in bulk specifically for the incentives market. To personalise it, you simply overprint the cover or supply a completely new cover, to include your incentive campaign logo and details of how participants can qualify. This is fine if you are running a campaign for your own salesforce or administration team. However, if you are one of many suppliers attempting to gain additional market share from a distributor (car dealer, retailer) who sells other people's goods too, you could find your 'catalogue' is the same as a rival's catalogue, bar the outer cover, thereby negating any competitive advantage in running the incentive scheme.

Bespoke catalogues are a better answer, but you need to have a participant universe of at least 10,000 to make it viable. The production cost of the catalogue could be more than the reward budget and certainly more than any incremental profit from the incentive programme.

Where there's a will ...

There are ingenious ways to get around the inherent problems with merchandise catalogues, all of which are valid.

Table 8.1 Problems and solutions

Problem	Solution
• Limited range	• Promote a few key items and simply list other related products as text
• Cost of catalogues	• Build the cost into the participant reward points
• Delivery delays	• Set up a hotline for telephone claimants
• Lack of client branding	• Personalise the cover
• Unbranded goods	• Emphasise value for money
• Goods too expensive for the campaign rules	• Earmark expensive items as 'star prizes', awarded mid campaign

Most of the disadvantages of catalogues are to do with presentation. Each audience needs to be considered separately and the appropriate merchandise catalogue chosen. Perhaps the most important characteristic of catalogues to acknowledge is that they are a very blunt incentive mechanism designed to appeal to a wide cross-section. They usually contain a varied range of items to attract the widest possible band of participants. But in doing so they can become untargeted and impersonal.

When to use catalogues

Catalogues do have their uses, but they are more shotgun than rifle, if they are being used as an incentive reward mechanism.

1. Small universe of participants

Provided the catalogue has been produced by the incentive supplier in large quantities, you can usually buy a good quality colour catalogue at a low unit price, even if you have just a small number of participants.

If you are setting up an incentive scheme for fewer than 100 potential participants, a catalogue with an accompanying letter detailing the reward points mechanism is certainly a rapid and cost-effective way to get colour promotional materials into the hands of participants with the minimum of administrative investment.

2. Diverse universe of participants

If your target audience is diverse in terms of geographic spread, range of income or volume of sales a catalogue can provide a catch-all solution as to what to offer as an incentive. Participants can choose items to suit themselves, within the range offered.

3. Loyalty building

If your aim is to establish medium- to long-term loyalty in the purchase of your product or with franchised employees, a catalogue can help participants accumulate points over a relatively long period. By involving participants' partners in the choice of item (by mailing to the home address and writing to both partners), you can extend the life of the campaign considerably and forge a strong bond between sponsor and participant.

Burger King Corporation

All 41,000 Burger King associates qualify for long service awards in the form of a selection of branded and customised merchandise appropriate to the number of years of service.

Participants build up credits over the years which can be redeemed for jewellery, sporting goods, household accessories, electronic goods and, in later years, holidays around the world. A toll-free (freephone) number is used for communication and merchandise selection.

4. Middle-band participants

If you know your top providers and have already decided to run an incentive travel event for them, a catalogue could be a good compromise for the middle-band category who will at least be able to earn some reward, however small. Perception that you can win something, however small, from the campaign is always important.

In broad terms catalogues are really for participants you do not know very well, but still need to incentivise in a volume-related sales campaign. Catalogues are a broad-brush reward solution in the absence of a detailed profile of the universe. In terms of effectiveness, they tend to work best in conjunction with other rewards or techniques (additional travel event, double points for the first month, quarterly bonus prizes, lottery element), because as stand-alone incentives, they can appear somewhat dated and unfocused to audiences who are well used to incentive programmes.

INVENT YOUR OWN CATALOGUE!

If you are not happy with the choice of items in an off-the-shelf catalogue or are worried that the spread of values does not reflect the earning capacity of points in your particular scheme (no point in having hi-fi systems on offer if the highest reward points achievable are £50), you could choose your own selection of merchandise.

This technique is often used for consumers such as petrol forecourt promotions where five or more levels of award are chosen. The participants choose an award depending on their spend. But the items on offer are hardly motivational and relatively disposable.

If you do choose your own selection of merchandise to suit your audience, you will face the same dilemmas as the big mail order companies.

> **QUESTIONS TO CONSIDER IF YOU CREATE YOUR OWN CATALOGUE**
>
> - What is the profile of the audience?
> - What items will complement their lifestyle?
> - How much will they be able to redeem from the campaign?
> - Will the items be available when they want to redeem?
> - Will there be enough of each item available?
> - Can I get a better price than buying the item retail?
> - What is the cost of delivery?
> - What is my policy on damaged or returned goods?
> - What is my policy on substitute models, alternative colours?
> - How do I deal with cross-border international winners?
> - What is my policy if someone claims they never received the item?

Many of these problems are to do with the decision to hold stock or not. One way around buying items up front in the hope that the participants will choose as you expect is to set up call-off arrangements from a range of suppliers as and when participants claim. However, there is always the risk that the item is no longer available at the price you set in your budget. The administration of setting up deals with ten or more separate award suppliers is not very efficient. What was originally going to be a 'simple' incentive offering a few dozen specific rewards suitable for your participants can easily turn into an administrative nightmare with the potential to cause more harm than good.

Catalogues are good catch-all reward media for a diverse audience which requires minimum administration. They provide the opportunity to promote the campaign with stylish colour material, even to a small group of participants at low cost per head.

However, because they need to appeal to a wide audience, the items offered tend to be bland, lacking in aspirational value and not of top brand quality. It has to be said that in the 1990s, catalogues can be perceived, among regular incentive users, as being old-fashioned and somewhat out of date as an effective reward medium.

SUMMARY

- Catalogues provide an inexpensive way to market desirable goods.
- But the time lag between claiming and receiving can be negative.
- If used for the right audience or as a first-time incentive, they can be effective.
- But they are a relatively blunt motivational tool with an 'old-fashioned' image.

9

VOUCHERS

Fair exchange is no robbery.

Proverb

We have come a long way from luncheon vouchers. You can now use vouchers in exchange for almost every conceivable product or service from child care to funeral costs. But why are vouchers so popular in incentive campaigns compared with cash or merchandise? They're cheaper. They are virtually instant. They are multi denominational. In other words they have all the flexibility of cash with none of the messiness associated with delivering merchandise. If 75 per cent or more of campaign participants choose vouchers whenever they get an equal choice between vouchers and merchandise, the perceived benefits must be considerable.

We covered the case against cash in Chapter 4. It is worth stating the case against merchandise so that we can consider vouchers in their true light. The territory will be familiar.

VOUCHERS v MERCHANDISE

Table 9.1 Cost of £100 incentive to participant

Reward Medium	Value	VAT 17.5%	National Insurance 10.4%	Total
Cash	£100	Nil	10.40	£110.40
Merchandise	£100	17.50	10.40	£127.90
Vouchers	£100	Nil	Nil	£100

It is clear from this example that, because vouchers under present legislation attract neither National Insurance nor VAT (value added tax) when provided as a benefit in kind, they offer distinct financial advantages over merchandise and cash when it comes to making decisions about reward media. The difference may not seem much for an individual, but if we assume an average reward spend of £75,000 in a bespoke motivation programme, by going the merchandise route, you as the programme sponsor are knowingly agreeing to pay taxes of £20,925, using this example.

There are many examples of companies using vouchers instead of cash to pay productivity bonuses or long service awards to maximise the possible payout to participants or simply to mitigate the National Insurance levy.

ADVANTAGES OF VOUCHERS

Speed of issue

One of the basic tenets of motivation is to provide reward as closely as possible in time to the desired behaviour so as to reinforce that behaviour in the future.

Provided you have written adequate claim procedures, vouchers can be as quick to issue as cash, often quicker as distribution does not depend on payroll routines. Vouchers are certainly quicker and easier to distribute than merchandise with none of the associated mechanical problems of transit damage, the participant not being at home at delivery time or simply not liking the item when it (finally) arrives.

Vouchers can be sent direct to the participant following a telephone claim. In some circumstances there may be sound motivational value in sending the vouchers to the local manager or line supervisor so that the vouchers can be presented in front of the participant's peers as a positive recognition opportunity.

Vouchers can be bought in advance and retained locally to use as soon as the desired improvement takes place. Many non-sales staff have benefited from voucher awards for achieving standards of attendance (combating absenteeism), hitting team productivity goals, improving customer service standards, improving vehicle care or rewarding efficiency suggestions. Even salespeople can be encouraged to take administration seriously using vouchers as the incentive. A major UK building society was concerned at the low levels of acceptance at head office of the new legally required Customer Needs Analysis (CNA) forms completed by its salespeople. If completion rates did not improve, the regulators of the industry could impose heavy fines or even take the salespeople out of the field for specific retraining.

A three-month incentive programme was devised, using additional training and vouchers to focus attention on this deficiency in the sales process. Participants competed to gain one of ten top places in a series of regional leagues with a specific amount of vouchers as the reward. There was a wide range of participant geographic locations and earnings.

The campaign was simple but effective. 'Right First Time' improved CNA form acceptance from 55 to 74 per cent with some branches achieving 87 per cent, with a minimum of administrative cost.

Multi denominational

Like cash, vouchers come in all denominations so they are flexible down to the smallest increment if you need to reward performance improvement exactly. Participants can add their own cash to the award if they wish to purchase items priced higher than their award. They can also receive change if there is a small discrepancy in the retail goods price.

You do not need to hold voucher stock unless you want to. Dispatch to participants can be by mail or through the line manager. Vouchers are easy to take home on the day the participant wins the award. They can even be spent on the same day, if required.

Flexibility is the key

But above all, vouchers provide the reward medium which matches ideally the personal aspirations of the participants. Because the participant chooses how to redeem the vouchers, you do not need to consider whether the catalogue reflects the profile of the participants or what items to buy in and promote for a specific campaign.

As we move towards a cashless society it is remarkable how many products and services can now be purchased using vouchers.

Staff Incentives and Performance Management Techniques

Here are just a few examples:

- Holidays
- Food
- Childcare
- Gardening equipment
- Books
- DIY items
- Health club membership
- Utility (eg gas) expenses
- Clothes
- Alcohol
- Hotel rooms
- Department store items
- Restaurant meals
- Sports equipment
- Music
- Television licence
- Petrol

It is now possible to pay for around 75 per cent of all regular expenditure using voucher systems. With vouchers sold at face value or less if purchased in bulk, they represent a most efficient way to deliver the reward. However redemption is an important factor for participants.

REDEEMING FEATURES

All voucher systems rely on prompt redemption in the same way that the economy relies on the banking system. Vouchers are no good if the retail assistants are not trained to redeem them. There is usually no problem with specific retail vouchers. If the logo on the shop front matches the logo on the vouchers, there is a high probability that you will be able to use them like cash.

However 'universal vouchers' are a different matter altogether. Not only do they cost more (upwards of 5 per cent of face value depending on volume purchased), there is always the potential problem that some retail assistants will not have been trained to accept the vouchers, causing embarrassment to both the award winner and the shop assistant. Universal voucher companies rely on the USP (unique selling point) of one voucher which can be redeemed in a variety of unrelated outlets. But like credit card acceptance, allegiances can change overnight.

One further problem is the spread of outlets covered. Some universal voucher providers claim acceptance in 'over 10,000 outlets', which should be enough for most participants' needs. However, in practice you may find that the geographic distribution of retailers in the scheme is skewed to the north or the south, or wherever, depending on the assiduousness of the voucher field salesforce during the previous year. This can lead to a significant number of winners not being able to redeem their universal vouchers without a lengthy car journey.

Popular vouchers

Each participant base tends to exhibit specific redeeming characteristics, given an open choice of retail vouchers, although there are some common features.

In the UK, Marks & Spencer (high quality clothes/food retailer) and Thomas Cook (holidays) are always highly placed and represent together at least 20 per cent of the total retail voucher market. This supports the view that if positioned properly, participants will use vouchers to reward themselves in aspirational ways rather than simply fund everyday expenses. You can encourage this by offering only those vouchers which can be redeemed for high quality goods or aspirational items.

But this is not always the case. Voucher choice often reflects the state of the economy, so in recessionary times vouchers are often used as cash substitutes. This is evident in the growth during the early 1990s of utility vouchers, food retailer vouchers and petrol vouchers. However, as the economy recovers, such options tend to be less popular.

DISADVANTAGES OF VOUCHERS

One possible disadvantage of using vouchers is cash flow. Because vouchers are the equivalent of cash as far as retailers are concerned, vouchers need to be purchased up front. No one can predict the success of an incentive programme or the choices the winners will make at the outset of a campaign. This leads to building stock at irregular intervals during the programme to fulfil requests. You could be left holding non returnable stock if you buy too much of one type too early. This problem can be solved by buying through an incentive house which habitually stocks all the leading vouchers and keeps a rolling selection available.

ADMINISTRATION

Voucher administration needs careful planning if you have a large universe of participants. The combination of a wide range of retail vouchers and making them available in small denominations results in a highly complex tracking procedure that needs to be as tight as any payroll system.

The key features of such a system are:

1. each participant needs a unique number code;
2. each voucher needs a unique number code;
3. each allocation needs to be dated.

From the sponsor's point of view, you need to be able to track which voucher was sent to which participant on any designated date. This enables you to prove vouchers were actually dispatched and received (if you use a recorded delivery service) if a query arises. The participant needs to be able to identify whether a voucher request has been actioned and, if so, where and when it was dispatched.

With most voucher supplies discounts are based on achieving bulk purchase thresholds. By tracking voucher redemptions on a daily basis, you may be able to qualify for higher overall discounts by buying stock forward to push you into the higher discount bracket, even if you have no immediate redemptions for that additional stock.

At some stage you may have to account for tax on vouchers issued to each recipient. By tracking dispatches on an individual basis the information will be readily available so that tax paid certificates can be issued to participants promptly and accurately.

VOUCHER PROMOTION

One of the great advantages of merchandise catalogues is colour pictures of the goods on offer. Vouchers by themselves are little more than alternative paper money. There is always the danger that voucher incentives will fall flat because there is too much emphasis on the feature (easy exchange medium) and not enough on the benefit (what they buy). In the final analysis a voucher is only a means to an end. It enables you to obtain the reward you want as quickly as possible. In itself, a voucher is a pretty dull piece of paper.

So, when you come to promote vouchers as part of an incentive campaign:

1. Concentrate on what the vouchers can be exchanged for.
2. Emphasise the wide choice.
3. Emphasise the speed of redemption, ie immediate.
4. Emphasise how easy they are to redeem locally.
5. Emphasise their collectability – the save-up-for-something-big feature.

It is noticeable that universal vouchers tend to feature strongly the range of retail outlets they cover, rather than what they can be redeemed for. Some companies offer a personalisation service to overprint an existing retail outlets brochure. This is nonsense. Participants only need to know where they can redeem their vouchers (or bonds as they call them) as mechanical information. The important benefit is what they can buy, so emphasise the reward not the delivery system.

'DESIGNER AWARDS'

On both sides of the Atlantic, there are many examples of delivering reward in unusual ways.

One approach is to follow the logic of offering as wide a choice as possible by simply allowing participants to accumulate points and for them to choose exactly what they want. Participants then ring a telephone hot line to obtain a quote on an item or service of their choice. It could be a specific holiday, having the house decorated, tickets for an opera, getting the car valeted, a meal for two at a top restaurant. The ideas are unlimited. The essential point is that participants design their own reward and work towards a personal goal.

'Designer awards', as they are known, are increasing in popularity as people become more individual in their needs and circumstances. Not everyone lives in a nuclear family environment. In promotional terms, spelling out the unlimited choice concept needs to be done clearly, showing examples of what designer awards are possible with perhaps ballpark prices. Experience shows that even by offering unlimited choice, you still find 75 per cent or so of the participants choosing the voucher route. But the unusual ideas generated by the remaining 25 per cent provide superb promotional stories to market to the participant database to prompt more imaginative redemption.

The Argos concept

An alternative delivery system in the UK is operated by Argos. Argos is a shopping catalogue company with retail outlets where consumers can buy goods or participant redeemers can pick up their goods. This makes an Argos voucher a useful incentive mechanism. Participants are sent a wide-ranging colour catalogue. Points are accumulated in the normal way and paid out in Argos vouchers. To redeem them, participants drive off to their local Argos store to pick up their chosen item. The Argos catalogue system combines the advantages of catalogues with the advantages of vouchers, thereby eliminating the delivery delay problem and the onerous redemption systems associated with ordinary merchandise schemes.

DEVELOPING TECHNOLOGY

However, the image of a consumer catalogue and the range of goods (rather than goods and services) may not suit all participants to the same degree.

Vouchers are now the preferred way to redeem incentive campaign rewards for most participants because they are as flexible as cash, and can be redeemed quickly and locally. The plethora of retail and service vouchers now available means that virtually anything in a merchandise catalogue can be obtained through a voucher system.

Vouchers

As technology develops, cable TV and home shopping concepts could be other ways to offer reward choices and a speedy delivery service, rendering printed media somewhat obsolete. There have been experiments in the UK with a smart card system whereby participants accumulated reward points on a personal microchip card to be spent in retail outlets which are members of the scheme. It is certainly an exciting paperless idea – the next stage in the voucher concept – but there are still some problems to be overcome. The distribution of participating retailers is just one issue, not to mention who pays for the hardware.

But it is likely at some point in the future that participants will be electronically credited and able to spend those credits by phone or with a smart card as soon as the reward has been allocated. Until then paper vouchers seem like the best bet.

SUMMARY

- Vouchers do not attract VAT or National Insurance and so work out considerably cheaper than merchandise or cash.
- Vouchers provide instant gratification and can be exchanged for up to 75 per cent of all regular purchases.
- Beware of 'universal vouchers' which may not be as redeemable as specific vouchers.
- Ensure you promote what vouchers buy rather than what they are.
- 'Designer awards' are the next stage in offering ultimate choice.
- In the future, redemption may well be through smart cards, provided enough retailers can be persuaded to participate.

10

EVENTS

There's no such thing as a free lunch.

Milton Friedman

Merchandise and vouchers are in general individual awards which participants redeem for personal effort. However, reward does not always need to be something you enjoy alone or just with close family.

Hosted events can be a powerful motivational tool in promoting performance improvement. If the event is overseas, it becomes incentive travel (see Chapter 7). At home, the same disciplines apply but because they tend to be smaller affairs, the emphasis is much more on recognition than logistics.

But why run an event? What is its motivational appeal? Where do events fit in the panoply of incentive rewards or indeed general corporate communication?

There are several kinds of motivational event:

1. sales conferences;
2. weekend incentives;
3. individual weekends;
4. group activities;
5. staff parties.

Staff Incentives and Performance Management Techniques

CONFERENCES

Even though individuals may not have to qualify for the domestic conference (although many do have to), it can play a valuable part in the motivation and performance improvement strategy of a business. Yet all too often regular conferences only pay lip service to communication, fulfilling only one side of the bargain — the directors directing the directed.

Communication is by definition a two-way process. Even in the most cost-conscious companies, it is recognised that the financial investment represented by the aggregate loss of productive human hours away from the field and the costs of staging the event is money well spent.

As a motivational tool a conference serves many purposes:

1. To pass on strategic direction.
2. To create a channel for feedback.
3. To launch new initiatives.
4. To recognise top achievers.
5. To establish new working practices.
6. To promote teamwork.
7. To stem harmful rumours (they can deal with negative issues too).

The first thing to establish is what purpose the conference serves. It may act as a focal point for annual planning and budgeting to ensure all essential plans are completed in time. It may be vital as the only opportunity in a year to report from board level to junior employee on the progress of the company. It could be used purely as a gee-up device for the salesforce to recognise high achievers and spur them on to better things. It could be the culmination of a series of smaller managerial meetings where the decisions made are then cascaded down in one hit to the rest of the organisation. But, whatever the main reason, there should actually be a reason, not just habit or that time of year again.

If performance improvement = knowledge × incentive × communication, then the conference is not optional. It is essential for sound motivation.

Timing

So, when should you have a conference? The table below shows the number of conference bednights booked by Forte Hotels UK Ltd between July 1990 and June 1991. It is a good indication of conference booking habits in general in the UK market.

Table 10.1 The Number of Conference Bednights Booked by Forte Hotels UK Ltd, July 1990–June 1991

Month	%	Rank Order
July	7.3	1 November
August	3.4	2 October
September	9.8	3 September
October	10.7	4 April
November	10.8	5 March
December	8.3	6 June
January	7.6	7 December
February	7.6	8 January
March	8.9	9 February
April	9.6	10 May
May	7.4	11 July
June	8.6	12 August

From this analysis it is clear that most conferences are held in the autumn, with a second tranche taking place in the spring. Very few have conferences in August. This distribution suggests that the main rationale for holding the annual conference is to review the year and launch the next fiscal year's initiatives. (UK company years are usually January to December or April to March.) However, apart from August, there's not much difference statistically on a month by month basis.

But it does not follow that every company should run its conference in the spring or autumn. You should hold your conference at the most suitable time of the year to support the main aim of the exercise. Toy retailers tend to run conferences in the spring or summer as new stock for Christmas needs to be sold into retailers well before the autumn. Pharmaceutical companies and computer dealers work in a fast moving product development environment. Quarterly meetings may be more appropriate than an annual address. Financial services tend to follow the traditional annual reporting cycle of April to March, suggesting a conference in April or May to be ideal.

Conference content

Once the date and the main objectives have been decided, the next thing to consider is the content. But great care must be taken to build a programme to appeal across several levels, not just the level of those speaking. A board used to having its own way with very little dialogue down the line is likely to produce a conference akin to a party political television broadcast, with most viewers turning off. The converse is also true. If the job of organising the conference is given to a relatively junior executive with little feel for the corporate culture, you are likely to end up with a very enjoyable event full of sound and fury but signifying very little when it comes to content.

The content has to include a careful balance of messages to support the main objectives, and provide the opportunity to share ideas or at least show openness to a consultative approach.

A checklist may help the organising committee focus their thoughts on what sort of conference they want.

CONFERENCE CHECKLIST

- The main purpose of the conference.
- How to measure its success.
- Audience profile.
- Proposed length of the presentations.
- Political/cultural environment of the business.
- Five main messages in order of importance.
- Pace of the presentations.
- Overall style (dramatic, businesslike, chat show etc).
- Need to incorporate existing materials/logos.
- Any elements to be carried over to future presentations.
- Specific format requirements (videos, slides, autocue etc).
- Planning schedule/deadlines.
- Authority for signing off ideas.
- Budget parameters.

Events

By answering these questions, however informally, you will have gone a considerable way to condensing the brief for production specialists to consider. Motivational elements are important – it should not be purely information provision. This is particularly true of the choice of theme.

Theme

A conference theme is important for both content and style, as it helps to clarify the main messages and identify a particular dominant image for the audience to take away with them at the end of the day. Themes are very subjective. They work best if they are ambiguous and tie in with the current mood of the company culture or market. Here are just some examples of themes which have been used in a variety of industries between 1992 and 1995.

- Embark on Excellence
- Going Places
- Question of Quality
- Against Adversity
- New Horizons
- Breaking the Barriers
- Building on Strength
- Today, Tomorrow – Together
- Charting the Future
- Committed to Quality
- Driving Force
- Excellence Comes as Standard
- The Express to Success
- Facing the Future
- Theory into Practice
- Go for Gold
- Counting on Customers
- People before Profit
- Mission: Improvement
- No Compromise
- Who Dares Wins
- Ideas in Action
- Leading the Way
- Future Perfect
- Winner Takes All
- Satisfaction Guaranteed
- People Matter Most
- Service First
- The Bottom Line
- Winning Through
- Quest for the Best
- On Course For Quality
- The Power to Deliver
- Steps to Success

Most work best if they have some specific meaning for the company or its culture. In a sales conference environment where you may be launching a new travel incentive, some veiled reference to an exotic overseas destination in the conference theme can help to underline the highlight of the day in the memories of those who attended.

Structuring the conference

As with any presentation, whether verbal, printed or in conference you need to develop a structure to emphasise the main messages in the most efficient way. There are several techniques you may want to consider.

- **Syndicate sessions** Where delegates are broken up into smaller groups with a facilitator to discuss specific issues and brought back into the main conference to report on their deliberations.
- **Celebrity compere** Where a professional link person or TV celebrity introduces the various speakers and interviews the top executives, asking difficult questions the audience perhaps may not want to be seen to be asking.
- **Chat show format** Where speakers give their message in conversation with the compere rather than formally from a lectern.
- **Motivational speakers** Famous sports personalities, explorers, achievers of all kinds tell the audience how they managed to achieve so highly, providing strong messages of preparation, teamwork and dedication to the goal.
- **Audience interaction** Where each member of the audience can press a button by his or her seat to respond to general questions from the stage, as in a game show.

The day needs to be planned to provide peaks of interest to keep the audience listening. You may decide to save your best internal speaker until the session before lunch to end the morning on a high note and provide talking points for delegates over lunch. The notorious graveyard session after lunch (where the audience sleep off their lunch) should be targeted as a participatory or high interest session (such as the guest motivational speaker) to keep the audience engaged. If you do have specific information to present from technical departments, you should consider whether the detail could be a handout at the end of the day and the main technical message communicated as a video module in the style of news reportage. Too many conferences are spoiled by technical supremos who cannot present.

A keynote speech from the leader is often billed as the last item. In most businesses this works well, providing an all-encompassing view from the top in terms that every individual can understand. However it is not always necessary to have the top gun as the compere. In fact, it detracts from the keynote speech if a few hours earlier the compere has been talking about departure details or the arrangements for coffee. A professional link person is worth their weight in gold and they do not necessarily need to be a TV personality to command attention.

Motivational matters

In motivational terms, any internal or distributor conference should confine itself to matters of direct relevance to the audience, discarding any tendency to include 'head office' items unless they are necessary to an understanding of the message. The principle of 'What's in it for me?' is as good a guide as any to what to include on the agenda. If the item does not help to improve motivation or stimulate higher performance, you should question why it is on the agenda in the first place.

It has been said more than once that a great idea for a sales conference is to hire an empty hall and simply let the delegates talk to each other for six hours. That way they get to learn 'best practice' without interference from the stage. Recognising that delegates want as many useful ideas as you can cram in to the allotted time is important when you decide what content to include or reject.

Finally, there is always the opportunity to recognise top performers at a staff or sales conference, so some thought needs to go into what may be appropriate. It may be practical to show pictures or text of top performers on screen, get them to stand up and take a bow in their seats or even arrange for some of them to be officially recognised on stage. The key point is to ensure that the figures are correct, the pictures are in the right sequence and they are being recognised for the right reasons. Including the name of the representative from Swindon could all go sour, if he was dismissed yesterday for gross misconduct. The recognition on stage could be accompanied by the presentation of a plaque or certificate, but remember to have a photographer on hand so that the 'moment' can be recycled the following month in the company newsletter.

WEEKEND INCENTIVES

Weekend incentives at a top hotel or a stately home have become an integral part of many sales incentives to support a longer term incentive travel programme.

Typically the very top performers over 12 months qualify for an overseas travel incentive. But 12 months is a long time to keep the message fresh. Many companies add quarterly or 4-month mini campaigns during the 12-month cycle to focus effort on key cyclical activities (prospecting, specific seasonal products, quality processes) to keep interest alive. One strategy in terms of the reward is to set up a small hosted UK weekend which is a mirror image of the overseas travel event, to encourage the weekend qualifiers to strive for the end of year event. Clearly secondary rewards (vouchers, merchandise) can be built into the mini campaign for those who do not qualify for the event itself.

Although generally small, attention to detail for weekend events is important, particularly if there are fewer than 20 guests. Conversation can be awkward for a group who do not know each other so hosting the event is vital to its success. It helps to have a guest list, with perhaps a two- or three-line 'biography' to encourage a meeting of minds. The company hosts should take the lead through a welcome speech, full involvement in the programme, and a proprietorial approach to service and smooth organisation. After all, the guests have risen to the top of their particular tree and they expect to be treated as winners.

Opinions differ as to the type of programme to run. Should it be a go-as-you-please weekend, only meeting up with the other guests for dinner or should every moment be packed with incident and frivolity? As usual, the answer is a compromise.

A typical programme which works well might read as follows.

Friday	*Check in, individually, from 3pm*
19.30 hrs	*Cocktails in the bar, introductions*
20.15 hrs	*Dinner in a private room, low key cabaret*
Saturday	*Morning excursion or activity for everyone*
	Lunch en route
	Afternoon free for recuperation, using the hotel leisure facilities, preparing for dinner
19.30 hrs	*Private cocktails*
20.15 hrs	*Gala dinner in a different (more spectacular) room with memorable cabaret, music, dancing if appropriate*
Sunday	*Breakfast at leisure*
	Depart individually before noon
	(Or offer a light lunch, with final thank yous before departure)

With this type of format, there is an opportunity to get to know the other guests early on, but there is also time to relax on an individual basis.

GROUP ACTIVITIES

Depending on the profile of the winners, participation days or weekends can be a good way to reward effort and promote teamwork, particularly for staff or singles (ie those without partners). There are many options available, limited only by the imagination of organisers and the willingness of the invitees to participate.

Here are some examples.

- **Murder mystery** Where guests try to solve clues to a murder, by gathering evidence and talking to hired actors who stay in character during the entire event. This can be done as a dinner entertainment which begins at cocktails and ends at midnight, with a whodunit conference next day in the library after breakfast.

- **Indoor problem solving** Where teams are given information, some kind of objective and a currency resource to promote working together towards a common goal in competition with other teams. Usually dressed in some kind of theme ('You are all oil explorers ...'), they provide an entertaining two or three hours with plenty of opportunity to practise analysis and teamwork skills.
- **Outdoor problem solving** Where teams tackle a range of physical problems to win points in a competitive environment. Typically this could include taking apparently unrelated equipment (rope, barrel, plank, clock) and using it to construct a means of transport or pathway to avoid an obstruction. There would be points available for speed as well as efficiency.
- **Outward bound** Where individuals or teams tackle physically demanding tasks in the open air with the aim of exploring attitudes to risk, teamwork and physical hardship. Surviving a night on Dartmoor or rock climbing are just two examples. Recently this type of activity has had mixed reviews with the suggestion that it is actually demotivating for staff to discover their manager cannot read a map or suffers from vertigo. You need to be clear about your objectives and be aware of the potential downside ('I didn't join the bank to risk my life down a pot hole'). Safety is a key criterion when selecting an activity.
- **Sports** For particular groups who would be entertained by trying out different sports (archery, snooker, golf, clay pigeon, tennis, croquet, crossbow, bowls, car rallying, buggy driving, driving a fire engine, ballooning, the list is endless). Once again what you like may not be what your guests would like, particularly if partners are to be invited.
- **National sporting events** A common interim award in many motivation programmes is a ticket to a national sporting event. The growth of corporate hospitality packages to Wimbledon, the Olympics and the like is testimony to their popularity. However, it is important to retain ownership of the hosting element. All too often winners can remember what event they attended, but not who paid for it or what the achievement was. Whenever possible, book private facilities so the sponsors can take full credit for providing the reward in the first place.

Choosing the right activity for the right people is an art and can gel or split a group, depending on their willingness or otherwise to participate. In general, go carefully if it is a group of winners and their partners. An optional approach might be best so that those with a health problem can opt out and not feel pressurised, while others may simply not want to 'participate' with strangers so you need to be accommodating. Staff or singles are easier in that they generally want to participate, but take care to cater for all tastes. For example, if a two-day teamwork reward relies heavily on golf, some female participants may feel discriminated against.

STAFF PARTIES

Although discretional staff events such as the Christmas party, family fun days, new office openings, company anniversaries or other corporate events are not strictly part of a motivation programme, they are part of a motivational mind set.

We have all noticed at one time or another the discrepancy in quality between events for the salesforce as an incentive and an event organised by the company secretary to mark some corporate occasion.

Treating all staff with the same degree of sensitivity and courtesy is a motivational issue. As part of the motivational mix internal corporate events should be handled by professionals, be allocated a meaningful budget and have specific objectives. The benefit of an overall incentive programme or a profit share scheme can be totally undone by a penny-pinching approach to non-essential events.

In broad terms building loyalty, and establishing a reward and recognition culture for staff as well as salespeople needs careful attention to detail if the investment is going to pay off in the long term in terms of staff retention and the internal willingness to share best practice techniques.

Events are important

Participants may or may not have had to qualify for conferences or events, but even if they are not strictly incentives or rewards, they still present an opportunity to nurture a 'we can do better' attitude. By accepting the fact that company events are part of the motivational mix, you are building staff or distributor loyalty for some time in the future when you may need their complete support. If you fail to input quality for internal events (or interim campaigns

Staff Incentives and Performance Management Techniques

in the case of an overall incentive programme), you may not get the quality output from staff when you need it most. In blunt terms, you either care or you don't.

SUMMARY

- Events can be a powerful way to strengthen the motivational mix.
- Conferences in particular can resolve complex morale problems.
- Weekend incentives need just as much attention to detail as large overseas groups.
- Non-incentive related staff events should be as high quality as performance related events.

11

MEASURE, MONITOR, MIRROR

> Mirror, mirror on the wall, who is the fairest of them all?
> **Brothers Grimm**

HOW TO MEASURE PERFORMANCE

Now that the reward choices are clear, the next step is to consider how to measure performance, because someone, somewhere is bound to ask, sooner or later, whether the investment has paid off.

The three stages in this process happen to alliterate and this makes them easy to remember:

1. Measure – establish the performance standard.
2. Monitor – calculate how each individual or group is doing.
3. Mirror – tell the participants.

Of all the decisions you may make when constructing a motivation programme, establishing the criteria for performance improvement is usually the least attractive but the most important task. Without robust measures, you will never know whether it has all been worth the trouble.

Quality control

Operating standards manifest themselves in many ways. From the legal accounting procedures of auditors to keeping an eye on the daily receipt of incoming mail, all managers rely on some form of

Staff Incentives and Performance Management Techniques

performance reporting so they can gauge how well or badly their department or company is doing.

The modern quality standards discipline has a distinguished past, from the famous Hawthorne experiments of Elton Mayo, which first suggested that man expects more than solely economic gains to be a satisfied worker, to the total quality management principles of Deming and his disciples. The recent obsession in the UK with charters of all kinds (the railways, National Health Service, local government) and the vogue for BS5750 (ISO9000) registration is an expression of the awakening of this need for more accountability.

But how relevant are these measures to real people doing real jobs? Can so-called non-producing administrative functions ever be effectively measured? They can and they are. But before we start the benchmarking process we need to establish why support staff need measuring at all, apart from the occasional heart-to-heart with their manager.

Why bother to measure support staff?

For many years quality, particularly in service industries, has been both a necessity and an annoyance. With such an elusive objective – quality – it seems to many management teams that achieving superior quality is just a question of investing more money in product development than their rivals. Promotion helps to establish the new 'quality' product, but if you rely on administration or production teams to produce it, all that development and promotion could be wasted. When the customer eventually comes face to face with the product or service, if support staff do not reinforce the new quality image then the consumer feels 'cognitive dissonance' ('Did I do the right thing by buying this product?'). The more expensive the product, such as a car or a pension plan, the more uncertain the consumer becomes. Supporting the quality product with a quality infrastructure is a vital ingredient in securing the sale, not just for now but for any repeat sales.

A quality approach to human resources ensures that expectations are met and that the promise is delivered.

MEASURE

With any group of people, you need to decide four fundamental questions when preparing an incentive scheme or performance improvement programme:

1. What elements of performance should be measured?
2. How can they be measured?
3. Will successful achievement deliver meaningful financial benefits?
4. Are the data robust?

Elements of performance

In Chapter 3 we considered a variety of business problems that could be addressed, for both sales and non-sales groups, through performance improvement programmes. But now we have to bite the bullet and say what exactly we are going to measure. All measurements start with an initial standard from which future improvements can be gauged. The first task, therefore, is to set a standard.

Individual job performance is a complex combination of many tasks, some more important than others. In a non-sales or supportive environment you may need to think long and hard what performance standards you can measure. In a typical administrative job there will be a core of functions that constitute adequate performance:

1. timekeeping, attendance;
2. telephone skills;
3. keyboard skills;
4. clerical accuracy, numeracy.

All these functions can be easily measured either objectively or by the supervisor. But beyond these basic skills there is a raft of other attributes which make an average employee into a high flyer, regardless of the job grade. These are some examples:

1. Problem solving.
2. General 'can do' attitude.
3. Positive response to deadlines/peaks and troughs.
4. Team player.

Staff Incentives and Performance Management Techniques

5. Leadership potential.
6. Task orientation.

These skills are inherently more subjective but can be vital to establishing a relevant standard. All of them can be measured either by the supervisor or the individual's peers, on a simple scale of one to ten for any given period.

However, the important thing is to decide which of the many elements constitute the core performance criteria for that job.

For instance, a service engineer working for a national power utility carries out specific core behaviour patterns which can be regularly monitored, even though the engineer may not be constantly supervised:

1. Attendance.
2. Percentage of calls made on time.
3. Percentage of problems solved.
4. Error-free paperwork.
5. Additional sales.

You may wish to add a supervisor's category to award credits for general attitude or some other team player type of attribute. But if in doubt, particularly if you feel favouritism could play a part, stick to known behaviour patterns you can measure objectively.

Junior staff

A junior administrator working in a credit card company could have measurable job functions as follows:

1. Speed of keying in.
2. Accuracy of keying in.
3. Average length of customer telephone query.
4. Additional services sold to customers.
5. Timekeeping.

A team player factor could be added where peers vote each month for the person in their group who has gone beyond the call of duty to deliver customer satisfaction, although the weighting for this element should not be as high as for the objective elements, to ensure fair play.

Senior staff

Even senior managers can be set standards which can be objectively scrutinised, although they tend to be more to do with specific financial controls:

1. Retention rates of staff.
2. Expenditure control.
3. Regular reports on time.
4. Use of training support for staff.
5. Evidence of regular team communication.

Once established, the core behaviour standards need not necessarily be written in stone. In many industries technology is moving so fast that the key constituents of good performance could change overnight or the company may need to stimulate a specific approach to customer service. This would lead to redefining the key standards on which to base any performance improvement process. In practice the assessment of basic standards should be carried out at least once a year, if only to check that the measures are all still meaningful. There are many examples of a mature scheme producing such high standards in one area (attendance, clerical errors, telephone manner) that continued emphasis is wasteful. The measure has reached its optimum which means that it is time to examine other elements of the process.

So, once you have decided what relevant elements to measure, the next task is to measure them.

How practical is it to measure performance elements?

With infinite resources, everything is measurable. However, there comes a point when the cost of gathering the data outweighs the incremental benefit. It may be perfectly feasible to analyse the job descriptions of 10,000 staff, establish their key tasks, brief managers and peers to award points for successful completion, and issue everyone with an individual rating each month against the average achievement. But the cost would be enormous and too time consuming. It may be best to decide which elements of the performance mix would deliver the greatest incremental benefit to the company, if detailed performance measures were introduced.

Staff Incentives and Performance Management Techniques

Let us take an example. An IT company has many categories of contributor to the process of creating profit.

Table 11.1 Motivation programme participation plans

Employee category	Specific programme
Directors	x
Sales	√
Marketing	x
Administration	x
Production	x
Distribution	√

Clearly, in theory, all categories would benefit from a performance improvement process if the company is going to be successful. But with scarce resources it may be that by concentrating on sales (new business) and distribution (delivering the product) the resources can produce rapid incremental benefits, providing enough profits to bring others into the loop.

Total quality management consultants may argue that everyone should be involved in the reorientation process. In theory, this is correct. Attitudes are important, right down the line, but if the choice is do nothing because the company cannot afford a fully integrated scheme at present, it is better to do something. Performance improvement is the art of the practical rather than the science of following rigid principles.

Once you have decided which categories to concentrate on, you will have another choice. Which elements of current job performance can be measured now, without any investment in data collection or new reporting systems? Many companies embarking on performance improvement for the first time are surprised to learn that they already have the measurement systems in place. The trick is to reorganise the data so that it can be played back to the employees in a format they will understand. Administrative functions often have a multitude of performance measures known only to management. By communicating what these measures are (and what constitutes success in the eyes of the managers), the staff suddenly become aware of the real rules of the game. It is difficult to score a goal if the goalposts are always shrouded in fog. Usually, the eventual measures to be used turn out

Measure, Monitor, Mirror

to be a mixture of existing measures and a few new measures emphasising a specific operational issue. Together, the new overall standard forms the starting point for relevant performance improvement.

Delivering benefits

Before we set off down the golden road of perfect performance, we need to be a little wary of creating flawless behaviour but no profit.

Each improvement should have a financial rationale. Keeping the office tidy is a worthy performance improvement but is unlikely to produce any major financial benefit. Improving sales prospecting activity, producing more efficient keyboard personnel and creating fewer clerical errors can all be calculated in financial terms as producing a quantifiable benefit. It is true that 'better team work' or displaying a 'can do' attitude cannot be objectively measured in scientific terms, so with some measures a certain leap of faith is required. But whenever possible, underpin any choice of measures with a cost benefit analysis.

Sales example

The number of dial spins by a telesales person per month is in direct proportion to the appointments made.

If we can increase dial spins by 20 per cent in a given period, we will increase appointments made by 20 per cent. The normal ratio of appointments to sales can be calculated and hence the incremental revenue.

Table 11.2 Ratios of Appointments to Sales and Calculated Revenue

	Dial Spins	Appointments	Sales	Revenue
Without programme	240	10	4	£60K
With programme	200	12	5	£75K
		Incremental Revenue		£15K

Administration example

The percentage of breakages by a warehouse staff is in direct proportion to the warehouse operating overhead.

Staff Incentives and Performance Management Techniques

If we can reduce breakages from 10 to 5 per cent we can reduce the operating costs of the distribution function.

Table 11.3 The Effect of Breakages on Replacement Costs

	Breakages	Replacement Cost
Without programme	10%	£50K
With programme	5%	£25K
	Incremental Saving	£25K

Each example will be different. In many cases you may have to make an educated guess as to the level of improvement (it depends on the professionalism of the performance improvement programme). However, in most cases, companies underestimate the improvements actually gained and are pleasantly surprised by the eventual benefits.

Robust data

One final element in setting the initial benchmark is to ensure the data are robust. In other words is the information you are collecting credible? The more subjective the measure the more likely it can be corrupted through bias. If it is a key measure on which an individual's or a group's performance depends, the whole programme may be undermined. Collection of the data needs to be constant. If, for example, a monthly performance measure is a factor of three separate measures, what happens if one of those measures is not available? Do you use the two measures which have come in and ignore the absence of the third measure? Do you substitute the missing measure with an historic weighted average? Do you exclude that individual or team from the process completely that month? These problems need to be thought through before the programme is launched. If in doubt, remove that measure before you start.

By examining all these issues before establishing the initial measures to be used, you will find the monitoring and communication process much easier.

MONITOR

The monitoring process covers how performance data are to be collected during each measurement period so that change can be shown. It is a data management discipline which requires professional computer knowledge and logical routines.

Depending on the sources of data (one office, regional offices, suppliers, market surveys) and the format of the data (manual, diskettes, tapes, modem) the periodic data collection task can either be simple or very complex indeed. In an ideal world a single tape or modem download from one source drives the report. In practice this is rarely the case. Most company data systems are driven by payroll routines, so adapting the current system to provide data for performance improvement programmes is never straightforward.

The most practical solution is to write a separate program which can receive the data in an inevitable variety of formats. A key starting point is capturing specific data to identify the individual without which performance improvement cannot be measured.

Typical participant profile fields

To ensure that performance data about two separate participants do not get mixed up or mis-posted, we need to establish some unique characteristics for each individual record:

1. First name initial.
2. Surname.
3. Employment joining date.
4. Employee number.
5. Employee job title.
6. Employee job grade.
7. Location address.
8. Full or part-time.
9. Employment leaving date (if relevant).

With 50 participants this could be done manually. With 5000 participants, it would be impossible to keep track of every John Smith who joined, then left, then joined again as a part-timer. if individual performance ratings are going to be communicated it is vital to identify the right John Smith.

Typical performance fields

To assess change we need to track where we are now with where we were the last time we analysed the data:

1. Target.
2. Target achievement comparison.
3. Number of transactions.
4. Attendance percentage.
5. Quality threshold achievement.
6. Documentation error rate.
7. Items processed against target.
8. Mystery shop assessment.
9. Supervisor's rating.

Each individual will have a different matrix of performance measures. Those who belong to different job grades or regions may well be performing against different numerical criteria.

Administration skills

Those who have the job of collecting and merging all these data need to have specific file import routines, otherwise no one will ever be able to unravel the various sources (and dates) of data imported. The process is a mechanical one with no scope for deviation, but the more data can be merged electronically without 'human' intervention, the better.

Assuming both manual and electronic data have been gathered we can then progress to probably the most important aspect of a performance improvement campaign – telling participants how they are doing.

AN EXAMPLE OF MANUAL DATA ENTRY INSTRUCTIONS

Description: *Branch Profit Quarter To Date*
123 filename: *Week 1*

1. From within 123 open a file
2. Change the directory patch to B:\
3. Select the file (double click will open it) – wait for it to load.
4. Check total no. of branches on file by looking a the row numbers or using @COUNT (from..to). Make a note & compare with numbers from other files.

To add a new column with the per cent Profit figure as a value with no decimal point.
5. Click in cell E7
6. Press the + key
7. Press the arrow left key
8. Press the * key
9. Type in 1000
10. Press return (you have entered a formula multiplying the cell D7 by 1000)

To change the format
11. Click on range
12. Click on Format (at the top)
13. Click on Fixed
14. Click in the decimal places box delete what is there and type in 0
15. Press return or click OK

To copy to all other cells in column
16. Click on E7 (where you have just entered the formula)
17. Click on the brown hand smart icon
18. Click the pointy finger in E7 & hold – drag down a couple of cells and left into column D – still holding press the END key and then the arrow down key. Move back into column E at the bottom of the range and release. The formula will copy into all cells from E7 to E186.

MIRROR

Output is where the whole exercise becomes meaningful. Without regular information about changes in individual or team performance, there is no programme and there will be no sustained improvement. Participants need to be told how they are doing. Moreover, the management of the business need to know whether their investment is paying off.

To mirror back performance there are many media to choose from.

1. Letter A personalised letter can be produced, driven by the main software program, to show individual performance against the key tasks laid out during the launch of the campaign. It could contain one element of data — sales achievement against target — or several performance measures, depending on the complexity of the programme.

2. Bulletin Normally used for incentives, the same information can be dramatised and highlighted using computer graphics, overprinted on preprinted stationery. A skier going down a slalom with flags denoting percentage achievement of target, a galleon sailing around an island or a car racing to the chequered flag can all enhance the performance message, and help participants identify what they have to do to improve.

3. Wallposters Depending on the cultural environment of the workplace, rank order positions or achievement against prescribed job tasks can be displayed as a wallposter so that peer group pressure starts to work on those not pulling their weight, especially if it is a team-based incentive.

4. Screen For immediacy, performance can be 'called up' on desk-top information screens at will or sent as 'must read' messages. This approach allows the organiser to respond very quickly to performance improvements, allowing participants to discover the effect of their achievement as quickly as possible after the behaviour.

5. Regular magazine To enhance the importance of any improvements made, a more permanent format is a regular magazine which can highlight faces as well as names and carry interviews with 'top improvers'. As CD technology advances a desk-top magazine will become a powerful motivational tool for reinforcing mid campaign improvements and creating role models within each peer group.

Whichever medium is chosen, response times are a major factor in closing the loop between achievement and recognition of achievement. Programmes which launch well, but have no mid campaign follow through in terms of performance monitoring are not only less effective but wasteful of the initial investment.

Local management involvement

Like most central initiatives within a large company, local management need to be consulted about the style and timing of the performance communication so that they can support the central message locally.

They will need, in addition, to be sent detailed management reports about the performance of their own people, compared with the national or grade average, so that they can take corrective action or indeed publicly praise those team members who are performing well.

Setting relevant measures and being able to report to participants on their progress is what distinguishes a performance improvement campaign from a sales promotion. Most employees deserve more than just a short-term bribe, if you are serious about creating sustainable changes in the way a company goes about the process of creating added value.

SUMMARY

- Setting the initial measures needs to be done in the context of what is practical.
- Monitoring the progress of individuals or teams will help participants work even harder.
- Communication of performance during the programme needs to be as close as possible to the achievement.
- Involve local management so that they can support local performance improvements.

12

RECOGNITION SYSTEMS

Applauding success and forgiving failure ...
Charles Handy

No reward without recognition. No recognition without reward. In the first instance the sponsor misses a big opportunity by not squeezing out the last ounce of publicity and acknowledgement while in the act of bestowing a reward. In the latter case, recognising good performance without rewarding it will be perceived as cheap and cynical by most workforces.

By itself, a recognition system is often the poor relation in many performance improvement programmes. It is either an after-thought to the main activity of constructing the campaign or it replaces the campaign when budgets are cut. Recognition systems only work when they are integrated into the main programme. They grease the wheels and transform an average programme into an incremental profit earner for very little extra budget.

But what are they and why are they so important?

WHY RECOGNITION WORKS

If we revisit motivational theory, we can see several ideas tending towards the same conclusion.

1. Maslow's hierarchy of needs describes a level of need where belonging to a peer group and distinguishing oneself for a specific skill within that peer group is a basic human urge.
2. Henry Murray cites two of the *Twenty Basic Human Needs** as;

'To rival and surpass others ... To increase self-regard by successful exercise of talent'.
3. Cottrell in *Social Facilitation*† argues; 'when two or more people act together the intensity of their individual behaviour often increases'.

If we can supply something to feed these basic urges, performance will increase. Corporate recognition systems do just that.

TYPES OF CORPORATE RECOGNITION

Beyond the basic level of corporate survival, loosely termed as holding down a job, what drives comfort zone employees on is recognition by their superiors and their peers. Recognition comes in many media, both formal and informal:

- Memo from an immediate superior.
- Letter from 'the boss' (divisional director, managing director, chairperson).
- Certificate denoting technical competence.
- Certificate denoting above average competence.
- Trophy for top achievement.
- Lunch or dinner with superiors.
- Discretional reward for extraordinary performance.
- Story in the company newsletter or magazine.
- Private verbal 'well done' by telephone or face to face.
- Public recognition of achievement in front of peers.
- Public, industry recognition of individual achievement.
- National industry award for individual or group performance.

Within every performance improvement programme there will be scope to arrange things so that many of the above ways to recognise achievement can be built into the programme.

---

* Murray, H A (1938) *Explorations in Personality*, Oxford University Press, New York.
†Cottrell, N B (1972) 'Social Facilitation' in *Experimental Social Psychology*, McClintock, C G (Ed), Holt Rinehart & Winston, New York.

176

CLUB CONCEPTS

Within corporate incentive schemes, club concepts not only increase loyalty but provide many ways to recognise above average performance. But what do we mean by a 'club concept'?

Consumer 'clubs' have been around for many years with the aim of selling additional products to established customers with the propensity to buy. Book clubs are the obvious example. Any list of past and present customers can be consolidated into a club concept. The fabric of the club is usually held together via direct marketing techniques – a newsletter or magazine is the normal medium. Club concepts for staff or distribution networks are somewhat different, depending on how close the sponsor is to the potential members. For employed or self-employed salespeople a club is usually a structured annual incentive programme comprising a single big travel event at the end of the year, supported by shorter term tactical promotion during the year. Club membership is determined by achievement of a specific sales or quality threshold which triggers access to a variety of club benefits. Many can be simply 'hygiene factor' items (for example free parking at head office, new briefcase). Other benefits can be related directly to doing more business (free use of a laptop computer, secretarial services, appointment making service). The third group of benefits tends to cover recognition elements such as cufflinks, brooches, ties, ladies' scarves, certificates and trophies for the top qualifiers.

A Financial Services Club Concept

Most life assurance companies who operate salesforces which sell direct to consumers have some kind of sales club. Aimed at the top 25 per cent, specific thresholds of commission are set to divide the qualifying participants into tiers to instil loyalty, improve retention and provide peer group recognition opportunities. No additional remuneration is normally paid, but there are significant non-cash benefits offered.

1. Invitation to the annual UK sales conference.
2. Invitation to the prestigious travel incentive destination.
3. Gold, silver or bronze cufflinks.
4. Tie denoting gold, silver or bronze membership.

Staff Incentives and Performance Management Techniques

5. Certificate of achievement.
6. Specific editorial in the salesforce magazine.

Communication to the salesforce in total or to individuals always includes reference to their club status, and rank order tables of achievement are produced and distributed on a regular basis during the sales year, not only to recognise past achievement but to stimulate would-be qualifiers to qualify the following year.

DISTRIBUTOR CLUBS

Distributor clubs are characterised by contribution in the same way as for salesforces. Depending on purchases made from the manufacturer, individual dealers or stockists benefit from preferential joint marketing programmes or invitations to specific manufacturer-sponsored events, by virtue of the turnover generated.

Carl Zeiss Italiana

Promoplan, the Milan-based incentive experts, devised the Zeiss Club way back in 1985 (still going strong) to recognise target achievement among independent optical stockists, and to support the Zeiss brand image of high prestige and traditional values.

Three levels of membership were set up: member, honorary member and VIP. There were varying levels of recognition. VIP members, for example, received a silver membership card in a leather holder, which acts as a credit card to 'purchase' items from the Club Secretariat (a selection of merchandise and leisure services).

In addition, VIP members qualify for a prestigious event with partners (Monte Carlo, Venice, Capri), restricted to the top 40 stockists.

So sought after has the Zeiss Club become that some stockists feature their membership in their consumer outlets and advertising.

It is often difficult to prove that such recognition devices produce more incremental profit. The only way to do so would be to divide the target market in half and offer the benefits to one side only. However, it always makes sound commercial sense to concentrate your efforts on those most likely to support your products. Most 'clubs' are aimed at the top echelon of business providers because their loyalty can help you build market share more quickly than by attempting to be 'fair' to everyone.

FREQUENT BUYER/LOYALTY PROGRAMMES

Taking the business commitment logic further down the road to true market representation, frequent buyer or channel loyalty programmes tie in the producer and the distribution arm even more closely. By purchasing up to specified levels, credits are generated in a centrally held marketing fund to support joint or independent local marketing activity.

Epson

Epson were the world leaders in printers but they needed to raise their profile in the UK. They realised they could not outspend IBM in marketing initiatives but they could generate loyalty from a selected group of UK dealers. A quality standards programme was set up in which dealers could earn credits through achieving specific Epson-related performance standards in such elements as showroom, use of merchandising material, staff product knowledge and handling supplied advertising leads from Epson.

The credits gained could be exchanged for a wide range of business support services including direct mail, local advertising, exhibition display materials, marketing consultancy, and attendance at international IT conferences and exhibitions.

INFORMAL RECOGNITION

One of the hardest techniques to master is informal recognition – very often the most effective loyalty builder. In the industrialised West, particularly in Europe, formal recognition systems can be perceived by staff as an alternative to increasing remuneration and a cheap way of buying loyalty. After all, everyone can see that a few certificates and a lunch with the boss cost much less than a pay increase across the board. If this is the prevailing attitude, a recognition programme will do more harm than good. It may be worth stepping back from the morale problem, and examining how managers go about blaming and praising staff.

A workshop can be devised to outline the basic psychology of supervisor/supervised relationships and agree a series of informal recognition techniques — to build internal confidence and morale. Once the management and staff are communicating effectively in this way, more formal systems can be grafted on top as a natural expression of the new culture.

Recognition systems are not an inexpensive panacea for poor morale. Staff can spot an insincere management attitude instantly. So, such initiatives need to be treated with care and used in conjunction with other incentive, reward and performance techniques if they are going to be received at face value.

Club concepts are so widespread that some incentive agencies have set up specific departments to deal with club organisation for corporate clients. Bernard Krief Motivation, France, sells a 'club kit' to companies who want the loyalty but not the administration a club can generate. Through careful collection of members' data, a series of offers are developed to appeal to particular member types to ensure there is always a basic financial benefit of membership in addition to any client product loyalty. In general terms the club kit costs around £300 per person per year including special deals and regular communication. But it always depends on the particular brief and the frequency of contact required.

William James, the 19th-century philosopher, wrote: 'The deepest principle in human nature is the craving to be appreciated'. The message about recognition systems is that by giving people what they want (more appreciation in the workplace) they will give you what you want; better commitment and higher productivity.

SUMMARY

- No reward without recognition. No recognition without reward.
- Feed the basic needs to be recognised for doing well.
- Club concepts increase loyalty and help build corporate relationships.
- Frequent buyer programmes help to fund joint marketing initiatives.
- Develop informal recognition habits.
- Integrate recognition systems into wider performance improvement programmes to get the best results.

13

PERFORMANCE IMPROVEMENT: THE FUTURE

Development is always self-development... The responsibility rests with the individual, his abilities, his efforts.

Peter Drucker

The responsibility for staff incentives and performance improvement techniques does not sit easily in any single department. Behavioural science tells us that the motivation of an individual is a function of inner drive, habit and incentive. It is the job of the human resources department to recruit employees with appropriate drive and train them in the internal processes of the company to create effective commercial habits. It is often the job of the sales or marketing departments to provide incentives which can transform an average performer into a high performer.

However, it is rare to find a brief which encompasses all the factors that can make a difference to an individual's performance at work. Human resources will concentrate on retraining the individual and offer career advancement with a revised benefits package as the incentive. Marketing will assume that, just like consumers, the individual is a constant and that positioning a non-cash incentive with the right packaging will guarantee success – at least in the short term. But real human beings are much too complex to be taken in by a quick fix or even a slow fix.

The rapid development of database techniques in all areas of commercial life means that for the first time we can establish performance standards on an individual basis and track the change

Staff Incentives and Performance Management Techniques

in that performance at a relatively low cost. The measures set may not reflect the totality of job functions in their unending complexity, but for the purposes of assessing key tasks, we are already there. Even the professions are succumbing to regular monitoring of agreed standards. Surgical operations can now be video-recorded to ensure procedures are followed. Solicitors will be obliged to keep accurate records of time spent on various legal tasks. Within the public sector, traditionally the last group to take up new ideas, job performance monitoring has become the norm, with quality standards springing up as the key issue in the most unexpected places.

As the competition within the global market slowly erodes product differences, the added value element of human service, that only people can provide, will ensure people will continue to buy from people they like, if there is little difference in the price or the product. The definition of 'likeability' will revolve around the process of human interaction — how people are dealt with.

Employees themselves are no longer content just to eke out their hours until it is time to go home. They ask for more involvement, more information, more performance related rewards. They want to be involved in the process of creating value. When they are involved in the decision, the improvement in daily operations can be remarkable. But their reward should not simply be more money. There is a distinct performance dividend to be gained from examining current benefit schemes, looking at cost-effective non-cash options, being critical about internal communication of performance and investing in the company's biggest asset — its people.

In this brief guide, I have tried to examine how a manager can bring out the potential in every individual to improve their performance at work. Not all the techniques described will work for you. There is no magic formula that will be effective at all levels for every type of company. Cultures are different. Markets are constantly changing. You need to experiment to discover what works in your situation. But, above all, you need to let the individual participate in the improvement process. Employees do have the capacity to respond and change, sometimes in spite of what the company does. Only by experiencing performance improvement personally will they want to repeat it for themselves. As George Kelly, the philosopher-scientist put it in the late 1960s: 'No one needs to be the victim of his biography.'

INDEX

absenteeism 16, 24, 64, 140
administration costs 58
AEG, use of incentive travel 103
agencies, motivation 59–60, 123, 129–30, 180
Argos vouchers 146
Armstrong, M and Murlis, H, *Reward Management* 70
Atkinson, motivation theory 35
Autoglass 8–9

banks, customer service
  investment 19; and job enrichment 24; sales networks 21
Barber, Michael 12
benefits, age-related 93–4
  difficulty in analysing 77; flexible *see* flex plans; and loyalty 79–85; as security 78–9
Berlet and Cravens, on pay and performance 71
Le Boeuf, Michael 64
BS5750 registration 162
budget 55–61
  cost headings 58–61; and flex plans 82–3; incremental profit 56–7, 61; motivation schemes 11, 29; recalculation 60–1; set-up costs 57, 59, 60; setting campaign targets 57
Burger King, merchandise awards 134

car industry incentive programmes 8, 52
CBI (Confederation of British Industry) 18–19
chance, use in motivation schemes 47–8
child care vouchers 139, 142
  flex plans 88

Citizen's Charter (1991) 69
close-ended and open-ended incentives 44–6
club concepts 177–8, 180, 181
cognitive dissonance 92, 162
'comfort zone' 70, 71, 73, 74, 75, 176
commission 65–8
  inappropriate selling 67–8; prospecting reward process 67–8; rules for 67–8
communication, common errors 93
  conferences and 150, 154–5; of flex plans 92–3; mirroring back performance 172–3
company performance, research and data collection 17
Conference & Incentive Travel Magazine 129
conferences, checklist for 152
  content 152–3; and incentive travel 116–17; motivational value 150, 155–6, 160; structure of 152–3; theme 153–4; timing 151–2
consultants, and flex plans 85
  and motivation agencies 59–60
consumers, increasing power of 11, 19, 68
cost headings 58, 59
Cottrell, N B, *Social Facilitation* 35, 117, 176
cruise travel 124–5
Cuff, Max 102, 103
Customer Needs Analysis (CNA) forms 141
Customer Satisfaction Index 39
customer service levels 19, 140, 184
cyclical sales trends 21–2, 52

185

databases, for flex plans 96–7
Dawkins, motivation theory 34–5
Deming 162
dental insurance 88
'designer awards' 145–6, 147
distributor clubs 178–9
duration of motivation schemes 50–2

employee benefits *see* benefits; flex plans
Epson, loyalty programme 179
escalator incentives 46–7
events, and motivational mix 159–60
    non-incentive 159–60; problem-solving activities 157–8; staff parties 159–60
exit interviews 24

feedback 21, 37
flex plans, administration 96–9
    advantages 82–3; age-related benefits 93–4; consultation process 85–92; database format 96–7; difficulties in understanding 89, 91, 97–8; employee discussion of 93, 98; and incentive travel 121; introduction of 83–5; linking into business systems 98; marketing 89–92; and medical insurance 87, 94, 95; motivational value 99, 100; pension schemes 93–4; pricing 95–6; promotional media 90–2; and recruitment process 91, 100; and retention rates 84, 100; selection procedures for employees 97–8; stages of communication 92–3; training of administrators 98–9
Ford, M, Motivation Systems Theory 36

General Motors, skill development programme 39
goal salience 37
Greenbury Report on executive pay 83
grievances 24–5
group activities 157–9
guidelines, in drawing up incentive campaigns 53–4

health care 87, 94, 95
Heider, F, motivation theory 35

help lines, in setting up flex plans 89, 90
holidays, and flex plans 88
Hull, Clark, motivation theory 34

incentive programmes, duration 50–2
    rules and regulations 53–4
incentive techniques, all or nothing 47
    close-ended and open-ended 44–6; 'commit-to-win' 46; escalator 46–7; fast starts, fast finishes 48, 103, 112; individual-based 41–9; leaguing system 42–4, 49; personal bonus 50; points pool 49–50; rank order 50; sweepstake/lottery/raffle 47–8; team participants 49–50; total team performance 49; weighting performance 49
incentive travel 8, 10, 28
    accessibility 106–7, 120–1; charter options 111–12, 124; check-in arrangements 109–10, 112–14; and conference sessions 116–17; costs of 101, 129; definition 102; difference from package holiday 101, 109–20; 'dinearounds' 114–15; extended stays 118; and flex plans 121; forward planning of destinations 126–7, 128; gala dinner 117–18, 119; as group 102, 109; group fares 111; individual 121–2, 122–3; methods of enhancing 110–11, 118–19; and peer group pressure 102; popularity 101, 102, 128; post-event research 109–10; product factors 122–3; promise factor 103–8; promotion of 107–8, 128; qualification periods 102, 107–8; and retention rates 102; role of partners 117, 118, 119, 122; safeguards 127, 128; special excursions and activities 115–16; and tax 116–17; trends in 120–1, 122–3; use of boats 124–5; use of trains 8, 113–14, 123–4; use of video 119–20; weekend incentives 156–7, 160
Institute of Manpower 71
ITMA (Incentive Travel & Meetings Association) 102
Iveco–France 106

Index

James, William 180
Jennings, Frank 23
Jenson and Murphy, on pay and performance 71
job descriptions 27, 64
job enrichment 24, 183–4

Kelly, G 184

leaguing systems 42–4, 49
life assurance, and flex plans 87
loyalty, merchandise catalogues 134
and recognition systems 179

McClelland, motivation theory 35
mail order catalogues 130, 131
management, attitudes to motivation schemes 17–19, 28–9
performance communication 173
marketing, of flex plans 89–92
incentive travel as 102, 123
Maslow, A, hierarchy of needs 35–6, 175
Mayo, E 162
measurement of performance *see* performance measurement
medical insurance 87, 94, 95
merchandise, advantages and disadvantages 139–40
attractions as incentive 129; selection problems 136; without catalogue 135–6
merchandise catalogues 9, 10, 145
advantages and disadvantages 131–3; background 129–30; loyalty building 134; for middle-band 135; number of participants 134; old-fashioned image 130, 135, 136, 137; production costs 132–3; role of partners 134
Mercury Communications, introduction of flex plans 83, 85–9
Miller, motivation theory 35
mirroring back performance 172–3
money incentives 9–10, 15, 27, 28–9
basic salary 63, 64–5; basic salary plus commission 65–8; 'comfort zone' 70, 71, 73, 74, 75, 176; costs 73–5; criteria 74–5; disadvantages 70–5; executive attitudes to 72; lack of 'trophy value' 72–3; manipulation of 63–4; performance 71
morale checks 25
motivation, close-ended and open-ended incentives 44–6
education 12; incentive travel and 103–8; research into 15; value of flexible benefits 99, 100
motivation agencies 59–60, 123, 129–30, 180
motivation schemes, analysis of implementation 26–7
attitudes of management 17–19; budget *see* budget; management attitudes to 17–19, 28–9; negative attitudes to 50; overall view 29–30, 31; pitfalls 26, 27; profit potential 12, 13, 56–7; self-funding 55, 56
motivation theory 34–7, 175–6
motivational events 149–60
abroad *see* incentive travel
murder mystery events 157
Murray, H, *Twenty Basic Human Needs* 35, 175

Nolan Report 83
non-cash rewards 10
non-cooperation 64
non-sales staff, assessment of 22–3, 39–40, 162

objectives, isolating 38–40
peer assessment 41–2; quantitative 40–2
Orient Express 8, 113–14, 123
outward bound events 158

Paris 104–5
peer assessment 41–2
peer group pressure, and incentive travel 102; performance measurement 170, 172–3; recognition systems 175–6
pension schemes 85, 87, 93–4
PepsiCo Foods International 83
performance measurement 10–11, 161, 183–4
cost benefit analysis 50, 167–8; credibility of information 168; and developments in technology 165;

187

elements of performance 163–5; peer assessment 164; practicality of 165–7; quality control 161–2; for support staff 162; use of existing measures 166–7
performance monitoring
 administration skills 170; data entry 171; fields 170; participant profiles 169
performance-related pay (PRP) 64, 69–70
personnel inventory 19–25
presentation, of flex plans 89–92
 of merchandise catalogues 133; testing of 30, 31
pricing, of flex plans 95–6
profit, incremental 11–12, 13, 19, 56–7, 61
promotion, of vouchers 145, 146
prospecting reward process 67–8

recognition systems 10, 28, 175
 club concepts 177–8, 180, 181; distributor clubs 178–9; frequent buyer/loyalty programmes 179; informal 179–80; motivational value 175–6; negative attitudes to 179–80; types of 176
recruitment process, and flex plans 100
research and data collection 15–31
 guidelines 16–17; into company performance 17; job roles 27–8; mirroring 172–3; monitoring 169–71; performance measurement 162–8; personnel inventory 19–25; of previous motivation schemes 26–7; on shopfloor 25–6
retail sector 19
retention rates 16, 20–1
 flex plans 84, 100; incentive travel 102
rules, for commission 67–8
 for incentive programmes 53–4

Saatchi and Saatchi 91
sales staff, administration by 140–1
 and individual commission 65–6; objectives 38–9; prospecting

reward process 67–8; recognition benefits 177–8; research and profiling 20–2
share options 27–8, 86
skill requirements 16
skills training 37, 39
smart cards 147
SNCF (French Railways) 9
sports activities 158–9
staff parties 159–60
sweepstake/lottery/raffle incentives 47–8
synergy 11, 13

tax, on incentive travel 116–17
 on merchandise 139–40; vouchers and 139–40, 144, 147
tax-free income 69
Tennessee Valley Authority (TVA), 'Quality Alliance' 23
Total Quality Management (TQM) 2, 162, 166
Touche Ross 18
training 37, 39
travel as incentive see incentive travel

United States, incentive travel in 121–2

Volvo, incentive travel 8, 113–14
vouchers 130, 139–47
 administration 144; advantages 140–2, 147; Argos 146; child-care 88, 139, 142; choice of 143; 'designer awards' 145–6, 147; and developing technology 146–7; disadvantages 143–4; flexibility 141–2; popularity 139; promotion of 145, 146; redemption 142–3; and tax 139–40, 144, 147; 'universal' 142–3, 145, 147
Vroom, V, on money and motivation 71

wasteful procedures 25–6
weekend incentives 156–7, 160
Weiner, motivation theory 36
White, E R 72

Zeiss Club 178